Per Aimee Alessandra e Luca Giovanni.
Grazie Bella, mi fai sentire un uomo migliore.

Published by Ockley Books Ltd

First published 2015

ISBN 978-0957141087

Front Cover designed by Michael Atkinson,
Layout & design by Michael Kinlan

Printed & bound by:

Riley Dunn & Wilson Ltd.
Red Doles Lane
Huddersfield
West Yorkshire
HD2 1YE

JUVENTUS: HISTORY IN BLACK & WHITE

www.ockleybooks.co.uk

CONTENTS

CERA UNA VOLTA VIII

ONCE UPON A TIME...IX

BORN ON A BENCH: THE EARLY YEARS OF JUVENTUS...1

THE ORIGINAL HEROES: GIAMPIERO COMBI & THE QUINQUENNIO D'ORO............................7

NO PLACE LIKE HOME: THE STADIUMS OF JUVENTUS...15

ITALIAN ROYALTY: THE AGNELLI FAMILY..21

JOHN CHARLES & LA TRIO MAGICA..29

THE TIRELESS LEGEND OF BEPPE FURINO..41

THE BIRTH OF SOMETHING SPECIAL: THE 1977 UEFA CUP FINAL....................................49

GIOVANNI TRAPATTONI & MICHEL PLATINI:

THE KINGS OF ITALY...55

IN MEMORIA..62

TRIUMPH & TRAGEDY: HEYSEL & GAETANO SCIREA..65

DEFINING A GENERATION: THE 1985 INTERCONTINENTAL CUP..75

CONTENTS

ROBERTO BAGGIO, IAN RUSH & STORIED RIVALRIES..81

TRAPATTONI RETURNS & MARCELLO LIPPI DELIVERS GREATNESS........................93

MAY 5 2002: THE BIRTH OF A NEW RIVALRY...109

THE END OF LIPPI BRINGS FABIO CAPELLO BACK..117

CALCIOPOLI & A CLUB REBORN..123

SEMPRE NEL CUORE: ALE, RICKY & GIANLUCA PESSOTTO...................................131

ALESSANDRO DEL PIERO: THE GREATEST OF ALL TIMES......................................137

THE FIVE SAMURAI...159

THE ALESSIO SECCO ERROR & BEYOND...171

A NEW DAWN BRINGS AN UNBEATEN RUN...181

CONTE CONTINUES & HISTORY IS REWRITTEN..193

FOREVER ENTWINED: JUVENTUS & THE AZZURRI...203

ACKNOWLEDGMENTS..209

REFERENCES...210

CERA UNA VOLTA

Una panchina in Corso Re Umberto, uno del viali nobili del centro di Torino.

Vi si ritrova un gruppo di amici uniti dalla passione per il football, quel gioco cosi speciale, da poco "importato" dall'Inghilterra.

C'e' un' idea che li stuzzica: fondare una società sportiva che proprio nel football abbia la sua ragione d'essere.

I ragazzi studiano al Liceo Classico "Massimo D'Azeglio," sono istruiti e il più grande tra loro non supera i 17 anni.

La scelta del nome viene messa al voti. Prevale quello che, in latino significa "gioventù."

Nasce cosi lo Sport Club Juventus.

E il 1 Novembre 1897.

Loro ancora non lo sanno, ma hanno dato vita a una leggenda.

Nasce cosi, quasi per gioco, la squadra più gloriosa d' Italia.

❙❙❙

ONCE UPON A TIME

A group of friends gathered around a bench on Corso Re Umberto, one of the most prestigious boulevards in Turin.

They met there, united by their passion for football, a unique game recently brought over from Great Britain.

One idea alone was motivating them: to establish a sporting club which would solely be dedicated to football.

The youngsters attended Secondary School at the 'Liceo D'Azeglio' which specialised in classical studies.

They were well educated and the eldest among them was just seventeen years old.

The boys decided to put the choice of club name to a vote and the Latin word for youth prevailed.

On November 1, 1897

Juventus Sport Club was founded.

They were not to know it at that time, but their meeting on a bench had given rise to a legendary football club.

This is how the most glorious team in Italy came to life.

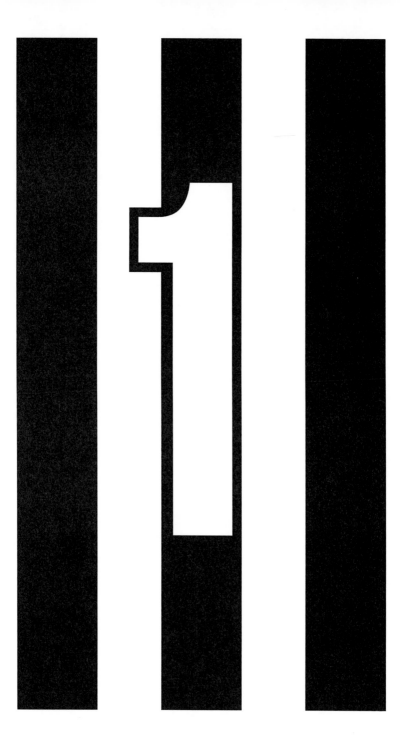

BORN ON A BENCH:
THE EARLY YEARS OF JUVENTUS

Football is a game of identity. Clubs are instantly recognisable through imagery, icons and by the colours they wear. Before the sport became omnipresent on television and the Internet, where fans were born and grow up supporting their local club, these identities were woven through generations of families and friends. Like many of football's grandest clubs, Juventus can point to the humblest of origins, far removed from the bright lights and multi-millionaire players gracing the sport today.

At the opening of the brand new Juventus Stadium on September 8, 2011, the Bianconeri held a ceremony which perfectly captured that history, and told the story of those early days. The club spared no expense in putting on a spectacular and emotion-laden display, and welcomed their supporters into this bright new dawn. Yet, looking past the hours of rehearsal and choreography, beyond the cheerleaders and former champions, the celebration of past triumphs and remembrance of tragic loss, it would be a moment that cost absolutely nothing which was easily the most priceless memory taken from the evening.

In the midst of all that glamour, noise and excitement, two men – surrounded by thousands of people and with millions more watching on television – sat on a bench and discussed their mutual appreciation of a club that both deeply love. It formed a wonderfully poignant moment, encapsulating everything that is good about Juventus, and indeed the wider landscape of Italian football. One of the two men was instantly recognisable to even the most casual observers of Serie A, the then-Juventus captain Alessandro Del Piero, a man who embodies all the virtues of what became known as 'lo stile Juve', the innate style of the club.

A man who spent the majority of his nineteen-year Juventus career letting his feet do the talking would, on this occasion, find the perfect words. Del Piero acknowledged his own place within the club's storied past, as he told those in attendance; "I'm proud of the important pages I have written in our great history. Juve have always been a wonderful painting and a great painting needs a wonderful frame like this."

More knowledgeable onlookers would have also identified his companion on that bench as the former holder of many of the records that Del Piero has since broken. Before Roberto Baggio, Michel Platini and Gaetano Scirea came to wear the black and white, Giampiero Boniperti brought the club out of the long shadow cast by city rivals Torino. Returning as President after his retirement, he helped Gianni Agnelli construct the team that won the 1985 European Cup, as well as being partially responsible for actually bringing Del Piero to the club. His words were equally heartfelt and met just as rapturously by those gathered as he said;

"My history with Juventus started on 4 June 1946 and I'm still here 65 years on to hug you fans and remind the current players of a famous sentence: For Juve, winning is not important; it's the only thing that really matters."

That last phrase is one Boniperti has stated many times, and is taken almost as the club maxim by many. As he uttered those words once again, a few well-informed fans may have even gone so far as to recognise where the two legends were seated, and like everything else on this most perfect of nights, the choice was no accident. It was the bench where students from the city's Massimo D'Azeglio school sat all those years ago, hatching a plan to found the now giant club.

They did so not with hopes of dominating Europe or even Italy but, just like we all do as children, for somewhere to have fun. The name they chose – Juventus – was also novel as, instead of being that of a town, city or district, is in fact the latin word for 'Youth'. Their kits would have been unrecognisable today, as they originally donned an all white shirt and 'plus-fours' combination, replaced in 1899 by a pink shirt with a black collar and tie. The club's first President was Enrico Canfari and they played at Piazza d'Armi, making their debut in the national championship on March 11 1900. It would be an inauspicious start as they lost 0-1 to the now disbanded F.B.C. Torinese.

A few years later, a set of circumstances and events lead to perhaps the most significant moment of those early years, the arrival of the famous black and white stripes so synonymous with the club today. The father of one of the players made the earliest pink shirts, but continual washing between games caused them to fade so much that in 1903 the club sought to replace them. Englishman John Savage, a member of that original team, was asked to reach out to his contacts in England to supply new shirts that would better withstand the elements.

The friend he contacted lived in Nottingham, and being a supporter of England's oldest professional sports club Notts County, he shipped out their own boldly striped shirts to Turin. It was no surprise that when Juventus were looking for the ideal opponent to inaugurate what was undoubtedly the most important stadium in Italian football history, the club eschewed the obvious options of Real Madrid, Manchester United or Barcelona, and instead invited English League One side, Notts County.

Juve have worn those Bianconeri shirts ever since, considering the colors to be far better suited to winters below the Alps than pink. Silverware soon followed and that same year they won the Coppa Città di Torino for the second time, beating Milan Cricket Club in the Final. Twelve months later they would lose again, this time to Genoa in the championship play-off, but soon they would deliver the club's first major trophy.

The 1905 season would be a memorable one for the fledgling club and they would end the campaign as champions for the first time ever. Unlike many of their rivals, the team called upon a core of Italian players, while other clubs filled their line-ups with English settlers. After comfortably topping the Piemontese group, Juventus entered the three-way national finals against Genoa and Unione Sportiva Milanese. They would be held to two 1-1 draws against the former, but beat the latter convincingly, recording 3-0 and 4-1 victories.

Those results would be enough to see them narrowly pip the Ligurian side to the title by just a single point. There was no tricolore shield to add to their shirts to mark the achievement as we see today, but the Football Federation did award the club a commemorative plaque. Juventus could finally call themselves the Champions of Italy. As was common at that time, they lined up in the W-M formation invented by Arsenal's Herbert Chapman, fielding Domenico Durante between the posts. In front of him, Gioacchino Armano and Oreste Mazzia were the full backs, with Swiss immigrant Paul Arnold Walty, captain Giovanni Goccione and Jack Diment of Scotland as the middle trio. The forward line was comprised of another Swiss national Alberto Barberis as well as Carlo Vittorio Varetti, Luigi Forlano, Englishman James Squair and Domenico Donna. The same eleven played every game and Donna also acted as the team's coach.

Later that year, Chairman Alfred Dick led an exodus from the club following some major internal disagreements over moving Juventus out of Turin. Several members of that winning side went with the Swiss textile magnate and formed Torino FC, giving birth to one of Italian football's oldest rivalries. The split was far from amicable and ensured that those early meeting of the city's two club's were laced with vitriol both on and off the field.

Carlo Vittorio Varetti took up the vacated role as Chairman following that schism, but between then and the outbreak of World War I, Juventus regressed. Living in the shadow of fellow Piedmont clubs Casale and Pro Vercelli, the club struggled to remain competitive, but the Great War did lead to yet another key event of those early years. With so many of the players called up to fight, the board decided they needed to find some way of communicating with them and decided to create the first in-house newspaper. The first edition was published on October 23, 1915 and it would be entitled Hurrà, giving birth to a publication still in existence today. Juventus would also be touched by tragedy as the Third Battle of the Isonzo would claim the life of Enrico Canfari, one of the founding members of the club.

The Bianconeri would make a triumphant return following the end of the hostilities, with players including Giovanni Giacone, who became the first to represent the Italian national team. President Corradino Corradini wrote the first club anthem, which was used until the 1960s. But this was a very different Juventus than the one we are familiar with today, with football still very much an amateur game and adhering to a raft of strange parochial rules. One such byelaw stated that players could only play for the town in which they lived, and the league was dominated by teams like Pro Vercelli and Genoa.

That would soon change.

THE ORIGINAL HEROES: GIAMPIERO COMBI & THE QUINQUENNIO D'ORO

It is the kind of story which fills dreams, a tale that one imagines would be almost impossible to sell to Hollywood's movie industry. The likelihood of cinema-goers suspending their disbelief until the hero had not only helped his hometown club to an unprecedented period of success, but went on to do the same on the international stage, coming out of retirement to captain his country at the World Cup. Trying to convince an audience that the tournament was also held in the nation of his birth, and that he would lift the trophy at the end before walking away from the game for good would simply never make the cut.

However, that is precisely the path which Giampiero Combi trod, enjoying an incredible career that very few men could ever hope to emulate. Born in Turin back in 1902, he joined the Juventus youth ranks and eventually progressed to the first team, making his initial bow in a February 1922 match against Milan. Aged just 21, the goalkeeper displayed incredible maturity and quickly made the position his own, going on to make a total of ten appearances in that debut campaign.

By the time the 1922-23 season ended – with Combi having started all but one of Juve's games – Genoa and Pro Vercelli had racked up sixteen league championships between them. The Bianconeri still had only won a solitary title, way back in 1905, and were some distance away from competing. That all changed in the seasons following July 1923, when a number of events occurred which changed the face of Calcio forever.

The league, which had previously been divided in a number of ways, was unified, whilst Edoardo Agnelli became President of Juventus. Rallying against the rule over moving clubs, Agnelli and defender Virginio Rosetta instigated what would become one of the first scandals of the Italian game. Playing as an amateur for his hometown club, the Pro Vercelli defender was idolised by the supporters, but took up a lucrative job offer from the Juventus owner to work as an accountant in Turin. With him in the side, it seemed a long overdue second title would finally be claimed by Juventus, but as Vercelli and Genoa – who would finish runners up – appealed the decision, the results of games in which the new signing had featured were expunged.

The incident, labelled the 'Caso Rosetta', became infamous as it eventually lead to the rise of transfers, wages and the advent of professionalism in the Italian game. Now often forgotten, it was arguably as big a decision as the Bosman Ruling in 1995, but it would push Agnelli's side down to fifth place and Genoa would win the league again. Once Rosetta was cleared to play for Juventus, however, a new era was born for La Vecchia Signora; an era with Combi at its heart, and the Bianconeri exerting their dominance to an unprecedented level.

In 1924, Combi would make his debut for Italy, called into the side for the first time by the great Vittorio Pozzo. It would be a match to forget however, as the Azzurri were demolished completely by György Molnár and Hungary. The 7-1 heartbreak remains the nation's record defeat even today. That result could not dent the confidence of the young goalkeeper, and he returned to domestic duties ahead of the 1925-26 season determined to drive his team to success.

His resolve would see Juventus return to the Championship play-off for the first time in five years, lining up against the previous year's winner Bologna. The first leg ended 2-2, while the second was a tense and nervous 0-0 draw. With no away goals rule, the two sides would lock horns for a third time, in a match held on neutral territory in Milan. Juventus would emerge triumphant, securing the second championship in their history, helped by the incredible goal scoring feats of Ferenc Hirzer.

The Hungarian striker smashed a scarcely believable 35 goals in just 28 games that term, and was ably supported by another 28 from Pietro Pastore. That they won the title was incredible, despite seeing their manager Jenő Károly dying as a result of a heart attack in the days between the final two matches. His compatriot József Viola, still a midfielder for the Bianconeri, would take charge of that key encounter and keep the job for two more years.

During that time, Rosetta and Combi helped Italy to a Bronze medal at the 1928 Olympic Games. Upon seeing Umberto Caligaris partner with them to complete an almost impenetrable defence, Agnelli would act once again. He signed a deal with Casale that would bring the latter to Juventus, and his decisiveness gave birth to one of the greatest defensive trios the game had ever seen. The legendary trio of Combi-Rosetta-Cagliaris was born, and Juventus would have its first true heroes.

The two defenders had constantly battled for one slot in Pozzo's national team, competing to partner the great Genoa stopper Renzo De Vecchi. Teaming up in Turin would be the making of both men. They would regularly feature together for the Azzurri; their understanding improving season by season. But it was arguably Combi who held it all together, perhaps the original superstar of Juventus, and certainly the pioneer of a great tradition of Bianconeri goalkeepers.

Unlike the giants found between the posts today, he was a distinctly average 1.71 meters (5' 7"), but he was strong enough to survive the kind of challenges that would be beyond more modern 'keepers. Due to that lack of protection, he was injured several times as a result of reckless collisions with opposition forwards, famously playing a game against Modena with three cracked ribs.

Over the course of his career he built a reputation for being amazingly consistent, rarely if ever having a poor game. Much of this was attributed to his incredible dedication to training, devoting himself to waking early every morning in order to complete a rigorous schedule of gymnastics and practicing the skills he needed on match days. He invented a routine of kicking a ball against a wall, then catching the rebound in order to hone his reflexes. His efforts paid handsome dividends, allowing him to set a record for Serie A's longest streak without conceding a goal – 934 minutes in the 1925-26 season – which stands to this day.

Following that 1926 Scudetto, Juventus would endure a somewhat dry spell, recording two finishes in second and two more in third place over the next four seasons. Those campaigns coincided with the league finally becoming unified in a single table. Just a year later, the Turin giants would begin a period of dominance which has yet to be bettered by any club on the peninsula.

Over the next five years, an era which would later become known as the Quinquennio d'Oro or 'The Golden Quinquennium,' was the first time Juventus was able to enjoy sustained success. Having looked on with envy as Genoa and Pro Vercelli each wrote their names indelibly into the early pages of Calcio history, this was when La Vecchia Signora would finally be able to do the same. She would win five consecutive league titles, a record run that has yet to be surpassed, and the only previous time to date that Juve has won more than two Scudetti in succession.

In order to accomplish this historic feat, Agnelli would provide stronger and stronger squads, using his huge personal wealth to build a team without peers. Carlo Carcano arrived as coach, a man praised as being "a great strategist and an excellent teacher of technique" by none other than the legendary Vittorio Pozzo. He was a devoted student of the Metodo system devised by Pozzo, which allowed players to thrive under both men.

Carcano was coach of the Bianconeri from 1930 until 1934, leading the club through the most trophy-laden period in her history, and even today remains the only man to have won four consecutive Serie A titles with any side. Remarkably losing just twelve league games during his entire tenure, he drew praise for his tactical ability, with Pozzo singling out "the discipline, teaching and organisation of matches demonstrated by a champion like Carcano."

Their 2–3–2–3 formation – forever immortalised on foosball tables across the globe – would perhaps be of greatest benefit to Luis Monti, an Argentinian player who would soon hold the distinction of having played in two World Cup Finals with different national teams. Playing as the centre-half, he would also arguably become the game's first defensive midfielder, as Carcano asked him to defy the usual attacking forays of that role to cover the pitch laterally and mark opposition strikers.

Monti dropped back in an unprecedented manner, providing cover to his full-backs and paving the way for the mediano role. He was clearly a rugged player, one of that generation's most fearsome tacklers, but had the technical skills to make him a standout who earned the nickname *doble ancho* – 'double wide' – due to the incredible way he covered the pitch.

Further forward, another Bianconeri legend and one of the first great strikers in Juve history, Felice Borel II, progressed from the Primavera to score goals at an incredible rate, netting 29 goals in 28 games in 1932-33, despite only being 18 years old. He would continue that amazing run over his twelve years in Turin, leaving Juve with 157 goals in 308 games, good enough to see him rank sixth in the club's all time scoring charts.

But this team was built largely on the excellence of that supremely talented back three. By the time the titles began arriving like clockwork, both Rosetta and Caligaris had matured to become almost unbeatable. The team conceded just 149 goals across those five championship seasons, compared to the 429 they would score themselves, thanks almost entirely to those three early icons. The former became a great organiser, taking over as captain and leading the side with distinction. He was an excellent reader of the game, often covering for the mistakes of his team-mates and saving them on numerous occasions.

The trio had now become central to both club and country, helping Juve take her first steps in the international arena, reaching four semi-finals in the Mitropa Cup which was an early precursor to the European Cup. However, as Italy prepared to host the 1934 World Cup and still clearly at the top of his game, Combi would shock both teams by announcing his retirement. Weary from having played over 350 games since his debut, he decided that, at almost 32 years old, that the moment had arrived to call time on his storied career. Despite boasting over forty caps, the legendary shot-stopper declared it was better for someone younger to take his place.

Carlo Ceresoli of Ambrosia-Inter emerged as the leading candidate, replacing Combi in the Azzurri line up, and playing a key role in qualification for the tournament. His display in the final game against Greece, a 4-0 victory, was widely lauded, and it seemed as though the torch had been passed. Yet fate would intervene as, on the eve of the tournament, Ceresoli would break his arm during training and obviously be ruled out. Combi, only with the team after Pozzo invited him to lend his vast experience to other players, would step into the breach once more.

The first match was on 27 May 1934 against the United States, with the Azzurri comfortably running out 7-1 winners, with no fewer than seven Juventus players in the starting line-up. From there, they would travel to Florence to face Spain in the quarter-final and, after an injury to Rosetta, Combi would once more pull on the captain's armband. Both he and opposite number Ricardo Zamora put on an incredible display of goalkeeping prowess in a game that, even today, is viewed as one of the roughest and violent in World Cup history. Ending 1-1 after extra time, a replay was held the very next day, Italy winning by a single Giuseppe Meazza goal, as both teams fielded vastly altered sides as a result of that barbaric first encounter.

Combi was again the star of the semi-final, putting on one of his finest performances to repeatedly hold Austria's 'Wonder Team' at bay. Their fearsome front line could find no way past him and Italy would again win by a 1-0 scoreline, booking their place in the final against a highly regarded Czechoslovakia. It would be game of stark contrasts, pitting the skillful artistry of the Eastern Europeans against the aggressive and tactically astute Azzurri, who had been ominously ordered to "win or die" by Benito Mussolini.

They would not disappoint Il Duce, although they played relatively poorly until Antonín Puč's goal sparked them to life. Italy poured forward, eventually scoring through Juve's Raimondo Orsi.

The goal was a brilliant piece of skill, as he turned quickly, beat a defender with a great move and rifled an outstanding shot past the helpless goalkeeper. The game went to extra time and Pozzo's better preparation and conditioning methods paid off, as Italy were much fitter than their weary opponents. Meazza ran unchecked down the right flank, as his cross was met by Enrique Guaita, who laid it off perfectly to Bologna striker Angelo Schiavio. He netted easily, and Italy had become world champions at home in front of an ecstatic audience and a delighted Mussolini.

He would reward the team handsomely, using the squad and its victory for propaganda purposes, and they too would enjoy unparalleled success. That triumph was reinforced by a Gold Medal at the 1936 Olympics and a repeat World Cup win two years later. It was one of the most dominant periods any national team has ever enjoyed and had Juventus players at its very core. In total, fourteen members of the Bianconeri contributed to those victories, becoming known as the 'Nazio-Juve' as the success of the two teams mirrored one another.

On the domestic front, Juventus would win their final league title of that era without Combi, who retired as he had promised, going out after captaining his country to the ultimate glory. His passion for the game remained and, thanks to his excellent judgment and intelligence, he filled various positions on the club's board of directors and the Italian technical committee. His life would come to a tragic end in 1956, dying as a result of a heart attack as he was driving in Imperia. Keen to be associated with the triumphant national team, Mussolini ordered the building of a stadium named after him in 1933, a home which eventually became the Stadio Olimpico, the current home of Torino FC.

But the club would suffer even greater lows following the bizarre death of Edoardo Agnelli in 1935. The seaplane he was traveling on hit a log, causing his head to fall into the still revolving propeller of the plane, and the 43 year old was killed instantly. La Vecchia Signora would stumble in his absence, with many of the key players leaving in the seasons immediately after that tragic accident. The loss sent the club into relative freefall with several of those great players leaving, and a clear line drawn under that period of dominance. It would be fifteen years before they would be crowned champions again, the longest title drought since the Agnelli family began their association with the club, and one which they have rarely even come close to matching since.

Combi's fellow stalwarts in that amazing defence both went on to coach the club, with Rosetta as player-coach leading them to their first ever Coppa Italia win in 1938. He was replaced after four years in charge by Caligaris, but neither man was able to repeat their incredible run of victories as players. His own tenure ended after just two seasons by another team-mate, Federico Munerati, and more members of that incredible side would follow in their footsteps.

Luigi Bertolini, Giovanni Ferrari, Luis Monti, Renato Cesarini and Felice Borel would all take a turn on bench, but anything close to glory escaped them all. Juventus would be forced to wait quite some time before dominating the peninsula like they did during the Quinquennio d'Oro, and that side should never be forgotten.

NO PLACE LIKE HOME:
THE STADIUMS OF JUVENTUS

From their 1897 formation until 2012, Juventus enjoyed something of a nomadic existence. Their early fixtures were played at both the Parco del Valentino and Parco Cittadella, before moving to Velodrome Umberto I for the inaugural Scudetto win in 1905. From there, they would move to Stadio di Corso Marsiglia, where they would remain until 1933, winning a further four league titles.

It was during this time that Edoardo Agnelli decided to build the small village of Villar Perosa in the mountainous region of Pinerolo. He moved his family there and the estate is still maintained by them today, including a private church where all members of the Agnelli clan are baptised, married and buried. From a Juventus perspective, the most pertinent addition was a football stadium which became home to the Bianconeri as they fled Turin during World War II.

The town remained as a training base until the 1980's, and even after that became the regular summer destination for the team's pre-season camp. Before long however, modern football – in terms of physical and financial demands – forced the club to join their peers in tours abroad. Prestigious friendly matches and build a better training facilities allowing for a more thorough preparation became essential, while allowing a greater number of fans to attend those games and increase revenue.

Yet Juventus would return each summer, holding an annual encounter between their A and squads, which was a game between the first team and the best players of the club's youth sector. Upholding the history and tradition which La Madama has made her own, this game became known the *Partita in famiglia*, 'The Family Match.' In addition to referring to the event organised by the Agnelli's, the name evokes the spirit in which it is held: the family of the players are almost always present and the club's Ultra always put aside their differences for the day.

The fans enthusiastically come together to provide support to their team, and whenever Juventus are in Villar Perosa, they always create excitement with street stalls popping up everywhere to an atmosphere that is both unique and extraordinary. Different generations of Agnelli's have sat on the sidelines, looking like proud parents who watch their children play in the local park, as the small hillside town comes alive once a year for the visit of one of the world's most famous clubs.

The club's next permanent home would be constructed at the behest of 'Il Duce' Benito Mussolini, as the city of Turin prepared to host the World Student Games of 1933. The stadium for them – along with the iconic Torre di Maratona – would be completed in a frankly astonishing eight months. Juventus called it home until 1989, and silverware would regularly be present as they secured seventeen Scudetti and seven Coppa Italia, while adding two stars for Sporting Merit – each signifying ten league titles – during this period.

Then they would move to the Stadio delle Alpi, designed by architect Studio Hutter. The 'Stadium of the Alps' was built to host matches for the 1990 World Cup and was host to Paul Gascoigne's tears in that year's Semi-Final. A combined Juve and Torino side would see off Porto 4-3 in a friendly to open the stadium, and the Bianconeri would add a further seven Italian titles and two more Coppa Italia triumphs in their latest home. The fans despised the stadium, which had serious visibility issues because of the running track, which never hosted an athletics event throughout the nineteen years of its life.

However, Juventus famously draw support from all across the peninsula, and this was one of the main reasons the cavernous delle Alpi was rarely full, its average of just under 38,000 nowhere near the capacity of 67,229. Indeed, there is no greater example of this than a 2002 Coppa Italia tie against Sampdoria, witnessed by just 237 spectators. The number of supporters spread across the country saw them become the most watched visiting team in almost every other arena, and resulted in a number of bold moves to play 'home fixtures' in stadia across the country.

The first of these moves came during the 1994-95 season, when the decision was taken to play the home legs of both the Semi-Final and Final of the UEFA Cup at San Siro. This move came after the combined attendances for the earlier ties against CSKA Sofia, Marítimo, Admira Wacker Mödling and Eintracht Frankfurt would have failed to fill the stadium.

Moving 126 km – some 78 miles – to Milan for the last two rounds was immediately rewarded as 80,754 people (then the UEFA capacity of the ground) saw La Vecchia Signora overcome Borussia Dortmund 4-3 on aggregate before the same number bore witness to a 2-1 Parma victory inspired by former Juve man Dino Baggio, who scored both goals.

Just over a year later, Juventus would reach another major final, beating Ajax on penalties to lift the European Cup for only the second time. By strange coincidence, that final saw them sell out yet another Italian Stadium, as the game was hosted by Rome's Stadio Olimpico and in front of another capacity crowd. Once again in that campaign, the Delle Alpi would disappoint, with just 55,000 people attending the Semi-Final victory over French side Nantes.

It would be this issue that led to another move as, desperate to show a sold-out stadium to the world, the showcase UEFA Super Cup that followed in December 1996 was held at Palermo's Stadio Renzo Barbera. After a huge 6-1 away win in Paris, UEFA Cup winners PSG would travel to Sicily and face Marcello Lippi's side in front of another full house. After UEFA segregation guidelines there were 35,100 looking on as Alessandro Del Piero and Gianluca Vialli ensured yet another trophy for one of the most dominant sides in recent history.

Juve would struggle in the final year of Lippi's first stint in 1998-99, and would only secure a berth in the InterToto Cup. Under Carlo Ancelotti's guidance they won the much-derided trophy, but not before once again making the move away from Turin. This time it would be the intimate setting of Cesena's Dino Manuzzi home, which was sold out for every fixture of the competition. Ceahlăul Piatra Neamţ, Rostselmash and Rennes would all visit the stadium and – such was the intimidating atmosphere – the Bianconeri would comfortably see off all three, conceding just one goal.

Even during the 2005-06 season, the Scudetto would be lifted in unfamiliar surroundings; the victory party was celebrated in an away win over Reggina, yet held at Bari's San Nicola due to the Amaranto's ban from their Stadio Oreste Granillo home. Despite the 866km (538 miles) distance between Turin and the Puglian city, once again it would be in front of a capacity crowd of almost 59,000. Del Piero and David Trezeguet would fire Juventus to their 29th title win before the Calciopoli scandal broke later that same year.

As recently as the 2010-11 season, when a U2 concert clashed with the Europa League qualifying round, Juve played Shamrock Rovers at a sold out Stadio Alberto Braglia in Modena (cap. 18,000), marking the latest instalment in a nomadic existence, undertaken in order to escape the emptiness of the poorly-designed delle Alpi. They would also return to the remodelled and renamed Olimpico di Torino for their victorious Serie B campaign in 2006-07.

In 2012, decrepit or unsuitable stadia were a major problem in Serie A. From the outdated Olimpico in Rome to the oversized San

Nicola in Bari, but most clubs had a plan, on paper at least, to move to a modern, purpose-built home. Many of these utopian ideals, such as the Cittadella Viola proposal by Fiorentina, were struggling to go ahead, whether through a lack of funding or assistance from local governments.

In failing to secure any of the recent international tournaments – despite numerous bids for both World Cups and European Championships – the country's football clubs were now beginning to realise they must fund those projects themselves or else face falling further behind their European counterparts as UEFA's Financial Fair Play regulations came into effect.

Almost all the stadia in Serie A are owned by the city council, and the clubs pay an extortionate amount of rent for the privilege of playing there – Napoli's San Paolo for example costing the southern side €600,000 per year, despite being woefully short on the modern amenities befitting a club set to compete in the seasons Champions League. As a result, they made just €14 million from match-day revenue during the 2011-12 season despite an average attendance of over 40,000 per game.

Those figures would make even Juventus, Italy's best supported club, jealous as they themselves averaged just 23,000 – the lowest in Europe's Top 20 Clubs during that same season, and only good enough for the eleventh highest in Serie A. Clearly this was hampered by playing in the Stadio Olimpico with its capacity of only 28,000, one of the first casualties of the Calciopoli fallout. The scandal – and subsequent drop off in income – forced the abandonment of a plan to redevelop the despised Stadio delle Alpi, but thanks to the work of Jean-Claude Blanc, a similar project was completed.

This new home would replace the aforementioned World Cup Italia '90 relic, and be built on the same site. It saw Juve forever cut their ties with the Olimpico, which will be renamed once again, this time for the city's other side, adopting 'Il Stadio Grande Torino' as its latest moniker. It marks the ninth permanent home for the much-travelled Bianconeri, and its reduced capacity of 41,000 much closer to the pitch than they were in the old stadium.

Despite costing approximately €120 million, the project has been largely funded by the sale of naming rights to Sportfive – who would in turn look to sell them on – for €75m and the €20m profit from selling some land to Nordiconad. This meant the club entered its new home in August 2012 at a net cost of just €25m, a quite remarkable piece of business.

The club was also able to make a number of deals with sponsors and associates for the new stadium, opening paths to revenue that would not be available had they continued to share their council owned stadium with Torino. Able to exclusively offer access to the Juventus brand meant far more to the investors, and it was no surprise to see Sony, Cartasi and Balocco shake hands with the club on deals as the opening day grew ever closer.

More than cost, profit or anything to do with financial gain however is a return to a stadium they can call truly their own, a feeling that has never truly existed at the Olimpico, delle Alpi or Communale. Whatever name ends up adorning this fantastic looking structure for Juventini, it will simply be home, at last.

———

ITALIAN ROYALTY: THE AGNELLI FAMILY

In a time before Arab sheiks and Roman Abramovich, football was – generally speaking – played with parity off the field. Clubs generated modest incomes and paid their players wages that were relatable to the average working man. As far as football in Italy is concerned, the end of that innocent age could well be traced back to the day in 1923 when Edoardo Agnelli took control of Juventus. The club, then less than thirty years old, and with just a single national title to its name, would be changed forever.

Thanks to the immense wealth at his disposal as owner of the FIAT empire, Agnelli would be able to permanently alter the entire landscape of the game on the peninsula. He established a legacy, which thanks to his descendants, is still evident today, as the family retains a controlling interest in Juventus, and with it, a prestige enjoyed by very few club owners anywhere in the world. The Agnelli name is perhaps, at least since Benito Mussolini forced the House of Savoy into exile, the closest thing to royalty to be found in Italy.

Edoardo himself was only 31 when he bought the club and, in just a few short years, would transform it beyond all recognition. First establishing a purpose built stadium and training facility at the family home in nearby Villar Perosa, he would then assemble a team which would dominate the Italian top flight in a way no side has ever been able to surpass. Between 1931 and 1935, they set records that still stand today, whilst simultaneously making a significant contribution to the Italian national team, which won consecutive World Cups in 1934 and '38, as well as winning Olympic Gold in 1936.

The name *Quinquennio d'Oro* is forever tied to Edoardo Agnelli, and signifies the first half of the 1930's, a decade in which Juventus won five consecutive league titles beginning in the 1930-31 season. They would also have a strong impact on the social history of the nation as a whole prior to the onset of World War II, as this was the era that the club began to be known as *la fidanzata d'Italia* – 'the girlfriend of Italy' – as teams began to be supported outside their own city for the first time.

All across the peninsula, the triumphs of Juventus were celebrated by passionate supporters who, according to Torinese historian Aldo

Agosti, "were the result of a particular set of factors: an unparalleled chain of successes, encouraged and accompanied by spectacular play, a decisive contribution to the national team that won the Jules Rimet trophy in 1934 and a clever image building nourished by a growing uptake of sports coverage in the newspapers." In short, the team became the first example of a perfect media storm that would be repeated exponentially during the 1990's.

Paradoxically, another reason behind why football supporters became Juventus fans during this period was recorded by University of Turin Professor, Giovanni De Luna. He believed that the club "represented then – and still does today – the alternative to the parochialism inherent in regional traditions and is considered an instrument of rebellion against local capitals." Being named after an idea, rather than a specific location, suddenly became a benefit as the nation rallied against the establishment of the Republic.

However, as quickly as that era arrived, its end would – as always seems to be the case where the Bianconeri are concerned – be swift and laced with tragedy. Agnelli died aged just 43 in a terrible air accident in Genoa, not long after the historic fifth title was won. Arriving in the port city, the seaplane he was travelling on accidentally hit a log floating in the water as it came in to land, causing his head to hit the still revolving propeller of the plane. It would not be the last time such pain was inflicted upon both the club and the Agnelli family.

Juventus would take seemingly forever to recover, as the departures of champions such as Renato Cesarini and Giovanni Ferrari added to the feeling an era was ending. They would finish fifth in the 1935-36 season, with Virginio Rosetta as player-coach. Despite adding their first ever Coppa Italia win in 1938, the club would limp into the post-WWII era in the shadow of their cross-city rivals, as the incredible *Il Grande Torino* bestrode the Serie A landscape of the 1940s.

For a time during 1942, with the league still not yet suspended despite the ongoing conflict, Juventus fled to nearby Alba to avoid the constant bombing of Turin, and would continue training there until the spring of the following year. In 1947, some twelve years after the end of the Quinquennio, a member of the Agnelli family – Edoardo's son Gianni – would once again be back in control of the club, and he would transform it beyond all recognition.

If Edoardo was the forefather of today's generation of oligarchs and oil-funded princes, then his son Giovanni – known to all as Gianni – must be lauded as Italian football's first instantly recognisable icon.

While modern players display all the benefits of multi-million dollar incomes thanks to platinum encrusted accessories and perma-tans, the always-dapper Gianni Agnelli established himself as the living embodiment of the phrase *la bella figura*.

With his wristwatch fastened over the top of his shirt cuff, and always immaculately dressed, Agnelli was heralded as a highly fashionable and a much sought after personality from the very beginning. By the time he sadly passed away from prostate cancer in 2003, the 81 year old had established a reputation, which was equal parts businessman, football lover and playboy, able to count David Rockefeller, Henry Kissinger and Anita Ekberg among his friends. Having spent his youth wasting money and seducing women at an astonishing rate, he eventually matured and begrudgingly took control of the family's business empire.

Agnelli revelled in the successes of FIAT, developing important relationships with celebrities and politicians as his influence and control grew. His visionary outlook saw him modernise the company, but what he truly cared for was the image of Italy as a country and, unlike many of his peers, the welfare of his workforce. The struggle to cope in harsh economic times saw his personal fortune fall as he observed those principles. With such a compassionate stance came an admiration and respect that transcended the apathy and loathing in which the majority of Italians hold the Bianconeri, as he became perhaps the one Juventino it was acceptable to admire.

Under his guidance, FIAT built schools and housing, gave workers extra money to take their families on holiday and provided them with lucrative pensions when their working lives came to an end. His business acumen and the intelligence he constantly displayed earned him the 'l'Avvocato' moniker, which, once bestowed upon him, never left. Literally translated as 'The Lawyer', the nickname was partially testament to his law degree, but also the manner in which he negotiated his way through the often tumultuous and forever bureaucratic world of Italian football.

As easily as he cut a swath across the politics and pettiness of Calcio, it was the inimitable style with which he always conducted himself that in turn became known as 'lo stile Juve'. Much like the New York Yankees under George Steinbrenner, Juventus players were held to higher standards than those at other clubs both on and off the pitch. Neat haircuts, no earrings, facial hair or visible tattoos, as well as displaying gentlemanly conduct were not just expected, but demanded by the club owner.

Again, much like baseball's Bronx Bombers, those same players were rewarded with higher wages, a hugely increased public profile, and had their image and privacy protected by the club at all times. Adherence to those rules would see even the most average players enjoy benefits they could never be expected to receive elsewhere, and those who moved on to other clubs would often speak of the perks they had sacrificed in leaving Juventus.

During the immediate post-war era however, those trappings had been unable to prevent the club from being overtaken as Italy's premier footballing superpower. Yet, what truly burned all those who held Juve dearest, was that it was cross-town rivals Torino – led by the mercurial talents of the legendary Valentino Mazzola – who had become the peninsula's best. It was then somewhat fitting that it would be Gianni Agnelli, easily the most eligible bachelor in Calcio history, who would take the Old Lady's hand and lead her to not only be Italy's most prominent side, but one of the world's best during his 56-year association with La Vecchia Signora.

Players and fans alike were constantly awestruck in his presence, while the press came to him constantly for quotes. He became the master of bestowing nicknames upon his players, often using them to both praise and criticise in equal measure. The 'Pinturicchio' moniker he gave to Alessandro Del Piero was initially coined as he was the understudy to the master Caravaggio, known at the club as Roberto Baggio. However, Zibi Boniek's 'Bello di notte' moniker was double edged. Meaning 'beautiful at night', it is often used as a measure of his prowess in evening European games, but Agnelli also meant his Polish striker would be a non-factor in the more tedious league games playing in the afternoon.

Perhaps only Michel Platini ever thought himself as Agnelli's equal, handing him one of the three Balon d'Or awards he won during his career with Juventus and telling l'Avvocato "here's something you can't buy, even with all your money!" Asked if it was real gold, the Frenchman quipped "if it was, I wouldn't be giving it to you!" The two shared a mutual affection however, reserving a reverence for one another that they rarely had for other people.

The respect afforded to Agnelli was due to an incredible record during his time in charge of the club. He led the team from one era of success to another almost seamlessly. His reputation remained intact whilst the 'Clean Hands' investigation wiped away many of Italy's leading personalities and the perception that FIAT and its owner were honest and true. Yet even his immense wealth and incredible lifestyle did not guarantee happiness, and the suicide of his depressed son Edoardo in 2000 scarred him indelibly.

Juventus was the only common interest the men shared, as Edoardo became a huge fan of the club during the 1980s. During an April 1986 encounter with Lecce, Edoardo came down from the stands and sat with Giovanni Trapattoni on the bench. Gianni had spared no expense when it came to his son, sending him to study at Princeton University. Following his time there he travelled through India and a meeting with Ayatollah Khamenei was reportedly behind his decision to convert to Islam. Seeing the changes in his only son appeared to make his father realise that he was not a suitable heir of the family's wealth, and his choices made the younger man ever more distant from the Agnelli's business empire.

In 1990, Edoardo was charged with possession of seven ounces of heroin in Kenya and later that year his body was found just outside Turin, on a river bed beneath a motorway viaduct. The bridge was known as regular place for suicide attempts and many observers close to the family believe that the tragedy of Edoardo's death accelerated Gianni's own illness and death. Agnelli was diagnosed with prostate cancer in 1997. His condition worsened and, after undergoing treatment in New York, it was revealed the condition was terminal.

Following Gianni's sudden death in 2003, the next family member would assume control of the club. Gianni's brother, Umberto, took the leading role for the Old Lady, already armed with a reputation as an intelligent football administrator over the previous years. Having lost his father when he was aged just one and his mother in a car accident when he was eleven, the younger Agnelli looked on as Gianni took on the dual role of FIAT chief and glamorous superstar. The latter's dominant personality cast a shadow over his urbane, witty, but retiring younger brother who earned a law degree and the moniker 'Il Dottore.' Having been President of the Italian Football Federation from 1959 to 1961, Umberto went on to enjoy a spell as a senator with the Christian Democrat party.

While Gianni was the car lover and public face of the family, the younger man was the bookworm and bean-counter who helped FIAT acquire the Alfa Romeo and Maserati brands, diversifying the company and making good progress in resurrecting the ailing giant. He would have less than a year and a half in the Chairman's seat, presiding over a fight back which meant the family kept their shares away from General Motors. He died in May 2004 as cancer claimed his life, just as it did his older brother's and, sadly, Umberto's son Giovannino. He was just 33 and succumbed to stomach cancer in 1997, causing yet more pain for those close to the Bianconeri.

Juve still managed to win the Scudetto in the one season Umberto was in charge, paying huge testament to fact that the family name had become synonymous with winning. That would happen again when, after the brief flirtation with Serie B, Umberto's own son, Andrea, assumed control of the club and restored Juventus to their place at the top of Italian football.

JOHN CHARLES & LA TRIO MAGICA

Serie A was suspended for two years towards the end of World War II, and then, in 1947 Edoardo's son, Gianni Agnelli, was appointed President. He would surpass the achievements of his father, starting with a superb 1949-50 season. Finally able to recapture Scudetto glory, the Bianconeri would net 100 league goals and win 62 points under new coach Jesse Carver. The Englishman had some incredible talent at his disposal including Danes Karl Aage Præst and John Hansen, the latter of whom would score 124 goals in 189 games for Juventus.

Giampiero Boniperti was also a member of that team and followed up by helping the club to a record tally of 103 goals as they finished third. A year later, with György Sárosi replacing Carver as coach, they would win the league again as Boniperti and Hansen built a superb attacking partnership. That win saw Juve join Genoa on nine titles, the most of any club on the peninsula, a record that the Bianconeri would make their own in the coming years.

As they looked to reassert themselves in postwar Italy, and emerge from the shadow of the Grande Torino side that dominated the 1940s, Agnelli would look to build his first super team. Deciding money was no object, l'Avvocato set out to build a side that would prove irresistible, capturing some of the finest talents of that or any other generation. His cause was helped immensely by the continued presence of Boniperti at the club, who was perhaps the epitome of the Stilo Juve implemented by Agnelli.

Before Alessandro Del Piero, Roberto Baggio, Michel Platini and Gaetano Scirea, there was Boniperti and the man is simply *the* Juventus legend. Born in Barengo, near Novara, he moved to lower division side Momo as a teenager, and it was there that he first came to the attention of Juventus. They were keen to sign him but, showing an insight that would feature prominently throughout his career, Boniperti insisted that both Momo and his home town club Barengo should benefit financially from the deal. He joined the Bianconeri in 1946 when they were firmly the second best team in the city and would quickly help to restore glory to the club.

Still not yet 18 years old, he impressed in youth level games including one in which he scored every goal of a 7-0 victory. He found himself drafted into the first team towards the end of the 1946-47 season. Despite Juventus once again finishing a distant second to il Grande

Torino, Boniperti immediately showed his potential, scoring five goals in just six league appearances. The following season, his first full campaign in Serie A would prove to be the most prolific of his career, scoring 27 league goals, and clinching the 'Capocannoniere' crown as the division's leading scorer. After just fourteen appearances for Juve, he also made his first appearance for the Italian national team, featuring in a 5-1 defeat to Austria.

The first major honour of Boniperti's career would arrive in the 1949-50 season, after the Superga disaster left neighbours Torino ruined forever. Juve finished five points clear of second place Milan, as the striker once again surpassed twenty goals, enough to earn a place in the Azzurri squad for that summer's World Cup. That competition ended prematurely for Italy, and despite quickly returning home, the experience appeared to spur Boniperti to even greater heights. Helping the Bianconeri to another league title in 1952, he passed the 100 goal mark in his Serie A career before his 24th birthday and scored a brace for a 'Rest of Europe' team against England at Wembley in the FA's 90th anniversary match.

Boniperti had matured wonderfully, become captain and had established himself as one of the greatest players in the club's history. Disappointment reigned however, as Juventus struggled in the league. Finishing as low as 12th in Serie A in 1955-56, two signings gave both the captain and his club a new lease of life. Having established himself as a prolific scorer and undoubtedly the biggest name in town, Boniperti would show his true class by readily accepting a switch into midfield in order to accommodate other players.

These would be no ordinary players either, as Agnelli pulled out all the stops and signed John Charles and Omar Sívori in the summer of 1957. In doing so, he created what became known as 'la trio magica' and looked on as Juventus enjoyed their most dominant period since the 1930s. The trio's first season together was the magical tenth Scudetto triumph, prompting Agnelli to adorn the shirt with the first Golden Star for Excellence, now a hallmark of Serie A's greatest teams.

Boniperti was ever present in the league, but scored just eight goals, and in 1959 Juventus won the first Coppa Italia of his career. Their third season was arguably the best, as they completed a league and cup double. Boniperti, having established himself as a centre-forward, now regularly found himself playing out on the right wing and would never again be such a prolific goal scorer. He developed a superb understanding with his new team mates, using his speed and skill with the ball to outwit opposing defenders with ease, cutting in from the touchline to regularly create goals for Charles and Sívori.

Boniperti won the last of his 38 international caps during that season, scoring Italy's goal in a 2-1 defeat to Austria, and as Juventus won yet another league title in 1960-61 Boniperti was no longer guaranteed to be an automatic choice. The final game of that season saw Juve beat Inter 9-1 in a farcical match, replayed due to being cancelled earlier in the season. Initially awarded as a win for Inter, the result was revoked, a move which almost instantaneously ended any title hopes the Nerazzurri harboured, and gave birth to a rivalry which lives to this day. In an extraordinary display of pettiness, Inter – then led by the inimitable Helenio Herrera – would field their youth team. Juventus ran riot as Sívori scored six, but for Boniperti it was the end. The illustrious captain walked from the field, handed his boots to an assistant and said, "Put these away, I won't be playing again." He was just 32.

Shortly afterwards, Gianni Agnelli brought him back to the club and he filled a variety of roles, eventually becoming President in 1971, and would hold the position for nineteen years. During that time, Juve won nine league titles, three domestic cups and all three major European club competitions. Boniperti then served as Managing Director before leaving in 1994 to pursue a career in as an elected member of the European Parliament. After Juve's involvement in Calciopoli, Boniperti was brought back as Honorary President in an attempt to rebuild the club's image. He continued in that role for some time, going on to see his grandson Filippo follow in his footsteps and graduate through the Bianconeri Youth Sector.

Upon ending his career in 1961, he had scored 178 goals in 444 Serie A appearances, both club records which would stand for nearly 50 years. His total of 182 Juventus goals was surpassed by Alessandro Del Piero forty-five years later in 2006, with his appearance record also falling to a striker cut from a similar mould. Yet Boniperti never once complained, telling reporters the head-to-head "made me more famous with young people than before. They knew me as President, not as a player and certainly not as a great scorer, now they do."

It is arguable that none of that success would have been achieved without the contribution of Omar Sívori who arrived in Turin at the same time as John Charles, for a then world record sum of £91,000. Unlike the other members of the 'Trio Magico', Sívori was as far removed from the two dignified gentlemen he is forever linked with as is possible. Short, tenacious, audacious and brilliant, but not adverse to football's darker arts, the Argentine was playing like Maradona before Diego was even born. His on-field histrionics were anathema to his classier teammates, with Charles known to go so far as slapping his strike partner in the face during a game just to calm to fiery play-maker.

He showed from an early age that he was going to be a truly great player and was spotted by Renato Cesarini, an ex-Juventus player who had gone to work for River Plate, in 1952. He would make his first team debut just two years later, emerging as a supremely gifted forward and blessed with a deceptively powerful shot. Sívori had already begun to develop a fondness for embarrassing defenders which made him popular with fans wherever he played. Known in Argentina as 'el Cabezón', which translates to 'Bighead', his usual move was to nutmeg an opponent, pushing the ball between their legs and running round to collect it. His repertoire also included dazzling feints and flicks, superb dribbling and powerful shooting from distance but he was also a tough tackler and worked tirelessly to win the ball back. He scored eleven goals in his second season with River to help the club win back the league title they had lost to bitter rivals Boca Juniors the year before.

They retained the championship the following season and Sívori was selected in the Argentina squad which travelled to Peru for the South American Championship in 1956. Along with Humberto Maschio and Antonio Angelillo, he became part of a lethal striking trio nicknamed 'The Angels with Dirty Faces' by the local press. After missing the first game of the tournament, Sívori scored three goals in five games to clinch the trophy and catch the attention of the world's biggest clubs. Juventus would win the battle for his signature, and all three strikers would move to the peninsula. That decision ended their international careers with the Albiceleste as the Argentinian FA, incensed by their abdication, banned them from playing for the national side ever again.

During the first four years of his Juve career he was simply unstoppable, scoring ninety league goals and adding another nineteen in the Italian Cup as his flair perfectly complimented the strength and power of Charles. The duo began the 1957-58 season in great form, as both scored in an opening day win over Hellas Verona, going on to net a total of fifty league goals between them as Juventus stormed to the Serie A title. A tale from that time centres on a match against Padova that, with Juventus already having done enough to win, saw Sívori awarded a penalty. He is said to have whispered to the opposition goalkeeper that he would allow him to regain respect from his fans and told him which side he was going to place his shot. The trusting stopper obligingly dived as he had been told to, only for Sívori to roll the ball nonchalantly into the opposite corner.

In 1959 Sívori scored a vital goal in the Coppa Italia Final, but the following campaign would arguably be his finest with the club. He earned the Capocannoniere title as the league's top scorer with his 28 goals shooting Juventus to another title win. They would go on to claim the double by beating Fiorentina in the cup final and Sívori would be one of a number of South American imports to the Italian national team. His Azzurri debut came in April 1961 against Northern Ireland and he would grab a late winner in a 3-2 victory. Later that year he scored a hat-trick in the 6-0 thrashing of Israel which secured Italy's place at the World Cup finals in Chile and his performances for the Bianconeri and Italy led to him being named the 1961 European Footballer of the Year.

That saw him become Juve's first winner of the Ballon d'Or and was a richly deserved reward for a man who had been instrumental in three *Scudetti* wins and two Coppa triumphs. But just as his great play was recognised, the great trio would be disbanded as Charles returned to Leeds and Boniperti retired. Without his great teammates to help, Sívori carried Juve, most notably in their European Cup win against Real Madrid where he scored the only goal in the first win by any Italian side at the Bernabéu.

Sívori had one disagreement too many with coach Heriberto Herrera and the South American was off-loaded to Napoli where he formed a fine partnership with Brazilian José Altafini. When he left Juventus, he was the club's second highest goal scorer, behind only Boniperti, despite playing just 215 games. He has since been passed in the list by Del Piero, Robert Bettega and David Trezeguet, with the Frenchman taking his crown as highest scoring foreign player too, and is the only player with a comparable strike rate. He enjoyed his career with the southern club and was regarded as a God by the football-obsessed Neapolitans, pushing his new team the closest to winning the league they ever came until Diego Maradona arrived.

By 1969, however, he was dogged by a persistent knee injury and, in another echo of what was to come with Maradona, his attitude was began to exhaust the patience of the Napoli board. Matters came to a head in a match against Juventus when Sívori was sent off for kicking a defender and, at an impromptu press conference afterwards, he embarked on a vicious tirade against his former club.

Sívori was punished with a lengthy suspension and abruptly decided to return to Argentina.

After briefly returning to River Plate he announced his retirement aged 34, but had surprisingly invested his wages shrewdly, working as coach only when he wished to. He would lead River Plate and Argentina before becoming Juve's chief scout in South America. He sadly died in early 2005, suffering from pancreatic cancer and passing away in his home town of San Nicolás aged 69. Enrique Omar Sívori will be forever remembered in the hearts of Juventini, a true great and a genuine legend.

If Boniperti and Sívori were key components, at the heart of it was Charles, the towering Welsh striker who was never booked or sent off in his entire career. That led to his nickname *Il Gigante Buono* – 'The Gentle Giant' – and he still holds the single season scoring record for Leeds. Before Ryan Giggs, Charles was the youngest ever Welsh international.

Quite simply, the man is one of the finest footballers ever to draw breath. John Charles was a wonderful sight on the football field; huge barrel chest, agile, quick and strong, a world class performer either in defence or up front and adept at playing in midfield or seemingly wherever else the fancy took him. A talent revered the world over, he managed to combine all that with a humility and generosity which has always made him a truly unique character.

"There should be a statue of John Charles outside every football ground to remind players what they can aspire to be"
– Michael Parkinson

Juventus showed incredible patience to capture him from the Yorkshire club, first showing interest in 1955, but not completing the transfer for over two years. During that time, agent Gigi Pernonace became a regular visitor to the Leeds training ground and befriended Charles while all the time reporting back to Juve what he had seen. The arrival of Umberto Agnelli, then only 22 years old, as President of the club signalled increased interest and he personally travelled to England to seal the deal. His arrival sparked huge curiosity, with a local businessman offering the player £10,000 to stay in Yorkshire.

Luckily for Agnelli, Leeds were in no position to turn down his advances, as a fire had devastated Elland Road and the club planned on using the fee they would receive to rebuild the stadium. Charles was represented throughout the negotiations by commentator

Kenneth Wolstenholme and his agent Teddy Somerfield, the duo combining their knowledge to maximise the earnings of both club and player. A lengthy negotiating process ended with agreement on a record fee of £65,000 and Agnelli had secured the services of a man who even today remains a household name among football fans on the peninsula.

The biggest stumbling block remained with Juventus as they battled relegation. That would prevent them from being allowed to sign a foreign player, but fortunately they remained in the top flight and Charles received £10,000 signing-on fee over the two year period of his first contract. His weekly salary was a modest increase on the English First Division's maximum wage, but a heavily backed bonus system and a luxurious way of life funded by the Agnellis would soon see him realise how lucky he was.

Rarely has a footballer earned such popularity across one nation, let alone the three that Charles counted as his homes. He remains to this day one of the favourite sons of Juventus in Turin and was welcomed back whenever he returned to the land of his greatest triumphs. Charles immediately captured the hearts of the Juve faithful on his debut, which came on September 8, 1957 against Hellas Verona. Goals from Boniperti and Sívori had made the score 2-2 when he arrived to slam home the winner. A week later against Udinese, he scored the only goal of the game and he hit the decisive strike in a 3-2 victory over Genoa. Securing three wins in your first three games is the stuff of legend and, above anything else, that is exactly what Charles was.

Many players have been famed for their versatility, skilled at playing in many positions, but it is inconceivable that any other footballer before or since has been quite so good in such very different roles. The great Nat Lofthouse was once asked, who was the best central defender he had played against and, without hesitation, named John Charles. The same week Billy Wright was asked, who was the greatest centre forward he had faced and, once again, the answer was John Charles.

> *"John Charles was the diamond, he made everyone*
> *else raise their game!"* – Giampiero Boniperti

For anyone who saw him play when he was at his peak in the late 1950s and early 1960s, the Welshman was simply immense. Charles was more than the proverbial battering ram. He was said to be blessed with the ability to hang in the air and his unselfish play won him many admirers. Such affection was fully justified for the contribution that Charles made to the history of Juventus and the wider landscape of Italian football. He would net 28 league goals in his debut campaign, lifting both player of the year honours and becoming the division's top scorer.

The facilities and luxuries afforded to the players were a world away from Leeds and Charles often remarked how Italian players took their careers much more seriously. With strict dietary requirements and no British-style drinking culture, many predicted he would struggle to adapt to the new lifestyle. It was never an issue however; the ultra-professional Charles very much embraced both the new outlook and the amount of time spent with the ball in training, in comparison to the fitness-based training he had experienced in England.

Away from the game, he would lean heavily on team mate Umberto Colombo, the family of the defender growing close to Charles's own wife and children. He was one of the only players who spoke English and the two men became great friends, opening a moderately successful restaurant in Turin at which they were regular guests. Fans flocked to see them there, hoping the striker – who released a number of albums – might treat them to a song or two as they ate. On the field he was equally revered, *La Stampa* calling him "a magnificent hunk of Welsh marble who bestrode the pitch like a colossus in the Juventus number nine shirt." They were far from alone and perhaps a piece by Giuseppe Melillo in a 1959 edition of the Corriere dello Sport best captured the adulation reserved for Charles. He eloquently described the player as:

> *"The greatest and most irresistible forward in our memory.*
> *He reminds us of the Swedish legend Gunnar Nordahl... the*
> *wonderful Taylor with his amazing style... the genial and*
> *intelligent Hungarian Kocsis... the spectacular Brazilian Pelé...*
> *the fine Sindelar of Meisl's Wunderteam... the fantasy of the great*
> *Alfredo Di Stefano... but frankly we cannot find any parallel for*
> *John Charles. The Welsh Giant is a completely different centre*
> *forward from the others. He is a new model; unique*
> *and unmistakable."*

Fresh from his triumphs in that debut season, Sweden and the World Cup Finals beckoned for Charles. It was to be Wales's finest hour in international football and remains the only time they have ever qualified for the game's most elite competition. They would play five games in the finals and lose just one, to the eventual champions Brazil. Charles missed the encounter with Brazil through injury and despite a heroic display, Wales would succumb to a Pelé strike which began his legend.

Back in Turin, Charles continued to enhance his reputation as a great finisher and as a truly adaptable player. It became normal for him to start a match at centre-forward then, when Juventus had established a lead, drop back and play at the heart of defence. Despite the close attention of defenders, the shirt tugging and obstruction, Charles somehow maintained his calm demeanour. Playing all 34 games in his second season, as he had before and would again, he scored nineteen goals in the championship. Twenty-three more followed in 1959-60 and fifteen in 1960-61.

Aside from a notable win over Real Madrid at the Bernabéu, the following season saw Charles finally run out of steam as he scored only eight goals in 21 appearances. That would signal the end of his time in Turin and the following summer he moved back to Leeds. Even that last season in Turin, however, had its peaks, notably Charles's performance at right-half in a European Cup game in the Bernabéu Stadium where Real Madrid were beaten at home for the first time in European competition. Returning to Elland Road also could not last and he soon returned to the peninsula with Roma for a brief spell, ending nine months later as he went to Cardiff City.

"He was a great champion and a great man. He is a person who interpreted the spirit of Juventus in the best possible manner and he represented the sport in the best and purest manner."
– Roberto Bettega

In the five years he spent in Turin, Juve won three *Scudetti and* two Italian Cups. Charles was Italian Footballer of the Year in 1958 and in both '58 and '59 he was in the top three for European Footballer of the Year voting. Overall, he scored an unheard of 108 goals in 155 games for the club. His later life was marred by poor business decisions, but the Agnelli family would often come to his aid helping him to overcome the financial disaster he made of running a hotel and a sports shop. They would also cover increasing medical bills as his health deteriorated.

After a protracted battle with cancer, worsening Alzheimers and a series of other illnesses, Charles passed away in February 2004.

Fittingly, Leeds United earned an unlikely draw at Old Trafford hours after his death and the entire footballing world mourned the loss of one of the all time greats. Charles's accomplishments and legacy are immense and he is clearly the greatest player ever to grace the red shirt of Wales. Leeds United's West Stand is now named The John Charles Stand in his honour and a bust of the great man looks over the banqueting suite. A street near the stadium was renamed John Charles Way and he was one of the inaugural inductees into the English Football Hall of Fame

"To be honest, I loved the admiration. If you're lucky enough to be born with a gift as so many people kindly say I was, then you might as well enjoy it. It's lovely to be so well remembered in Italy after all this time; maybe it's because Italian families tend to be so close-knit that they still show me such affection."
– John Charles

His accomplishments with Juventus led to him being voted Serie A's greatest ever foreign player in 1997, ahead of Diego Maradona, Michel Platini and Marco Van Basten. That the award was made 34 years after his last appearance in the league is testament to the lasting impression he made on the whole country. To hear chants of *'Gio-va-nni Gio-va-nni'* echo round the Turin stadium on his final visit in 2001 was simply astonishing. He may have arrived as the Gentle Giant, but when he left Italy, John Charles had been bestowed with a very different moniker – *Il Re* (The King) – and that is how he should always be remembered. Long live the King.

THE TIRELESS LEGEND OF BEPPE FURINO

In the pantheon of Juventus legends, there are almost too many eye-catching names to choose from when identifying the true greats. From global icons such as Roberto Baggio and Michel Platini to those like Alessandro Del Piero and Gaetano Scirea who are as synonymous with the club as the famous black and white striped shirts. All too often a genuinely vital player will be overlooked among this plethora of legends and that, in essence, is the story of one of the finest ever to represent La Vecchia Signora.

A cursory glance over the statistics of his career will show he scored just eight goals and earned a meagre three caps for Italy. When even the most modest of Juve players seems to receive regular calls to don the Azzurri, it would appear that Beppe Furino is the exception that proves the rule. But make no mistake; from the day he made his debut in 1969 to the day he retired, very few men have embodied the spirit and style of Juventus as much as he did.

Born in Palermo shortly after the end of World War II, the young Furino and his family moved north in search of work. His talent for football was quickly identified by Juventus and he spent his formative years in the club's academy. Unsure of how to best use him, he was sent on loan for two seasons with Savona in Serie B where he made 61 appearances as a distinctly average left winger. In an attempt to test him more fully, he was recalled and moved back to Sicily for a year.

After initially struggling to find space in the team, it was there in Palermo, a town he spent little time in but with which he admits to having "a special relationship", that he began to truly flourish. Coach Carmelo Di Bella, who had steered the Rosanero to promotion in the previous season, was a deep thinker and renowned smoker, revered by many as 'the Helenio Herrera of the South' for his stellar work both with Palermo and Cagliari. Just a few games into the 1968-69 season, he saw a gap for a defensive midfielder in his struggling side and thrust Furino, by then already 22 years of age, into the role. He would never look back.

Whilst he was learning this new role away from the spotlight, Giampiero Boniperti had, like most connected to Juventus, grown tired of Heriberto Herrera and his strict adherence to his movimiento ideology. After initial success, the inflexible, dogmatic approach of the man known as the 'Iron Sergeant' became unbearable and sweeping changes were made. Furino's displays for Palermo during the rest of that campaign convinced the President to bring him back to Turin and see if he could replicate his superb form as part of a brand new era.

Following a Coppa Italia appearance against Mantova, fate would conspire that the reinvented midfielder would make his Serie A debut against Palermo at the Stadio Communale. Juve quickly fell behind to a Gaetano Troja strike after just four minutes, but that sparked the home side into life, reacting furiously to gifting their opponents the lead. A goal from Lamberto Leonardi and two from Helmut Haller quickly restored their confidence before Furino would sign off with a rare strike. Just over ten minutes remained when he stole forward, collecting the ball at the edge of the box and scuffing an ugly left-footed shot into the bottom corner to seal the points.

From that day on he grew in his new role, his confidence and ability increasing year by year until it became impossible to imagine any other player donning the number four shirt for Juventus. These were the days long before squad numbers when each shirt was tied to a position and nobody personified their own more than Furino. Somehow in England it has become known as the 'Makélélé role,' while other descriptions include Eric Cantona famously dubbing Didier Deschamps a water carrier. Nowadays, the phrase holding player, or defensive pivot are regularly used but in Italy these players have described as a mediano for years.

A deep lying defensive midfielder, he was responsible for breaking up opposition attacks, shielding the defence and rebuilding the play; a task usually accomplished by giving the ball to a more talented teammate. Had journalist Gianni Brera not already coined the term – along with almost every other in Italian football – the position could easily be named after Furino, who became perhaps its most accomplished exponent ever.

He was fully committed to Boniperti's philosophy that winning was all that mattered and never gave up on any match. After a victory, he would immediately begin to prepare for the next, while journalist Vladimiro Caminiti described him as "the most evil mediano in Italy" in a TuttoSport column in 1973. Colourfully portraying Furino's playing style as like "gnawing on the skull of opponents and, when it comes to picking a fight, he is always prepared," gives us an insight into what life was like in Serie A midfields during this period.

There was still much work to do at Juventus however, and by the end of the season they finished a distant third behind eventual champions Cagliari. Furino had done enough to be granted a place in Ferruccio Valcareggi's squad for the World Cup in Mexico, making his debut as a half-time substitute in a 0-0 draw with Uruguay. It would be his only appearance, as Italy progressed to the Final where they were thoroughly outplayed by Brazil.

He returned to domestic action buoyed by his small part in Italy's best showing at the global showpiece since their 1930s golden era. Recognising that he belonged among the best players on the peninsula inspired him to push even harder on the domestic scene and he continued to carve out an unmistakable niche in the side. They would finish fourth in 1970-71, but the following season were crowned Champions and would repeat the feat a year later.

By now Furino was integral to Juventus and he would play a key role in their march to the 1973 European Cup Final, which should have been the crowning moment for Čestmír Vycpálek's exciting team. They swept all before them both at home and on the continent, easing their way past Marseille, FC Magdeburg of Germany and Újpest before coming face-to-face with Brian Clough and Derby County in the semi-final.

"Juventus are the finest team we have played in the competition so far but I honestly and sincerely believe that Derby County can reach the final." – Brian Clough

72,000 people were crammed into the Stadio Communale for the first leg and, despite a great start by the First Division Champions, Juventus would take the lead through José Altafini. The Rams would equalise two minutes later, as Kevin Hector embarrassed Dino Zoff, netting the first ever goal by an English side on Italian soil in Europe's elite competition. From there the game evened out and remained in the balance until Haller was introduced after 62 minutes, the presence of the German playmaker lifting the Bianconeri and just four minutes later Franco Causio restored their lead.

Altafini and Causio squandered chances to kill the game, the latter hitting the post. The real talking point, however, would be the performances of both Furino and referee Gerhard Schulenburg. The midfielder lived up to his reputation as a master of the game's darker arts, especially after he was booked in the first half. The yellow card meant he would miss the return leg and from then made it his duty to ensure as many Derby players as possible would also be unavailable for that game.

His tactics, though not in-keeping with the spirit of the game, would pay off handsomely, not least when Archie Gemmill received a booking of his own for a trip on Furino. That it was merely retaliation after the Italian had elbowed him in the face which somehow escaped the attention of the officials, and Derby captain Roy McFarland would join the Scotsman in missing the game after being cautioned himself. Furino would continue to systematically trip, hold and obstruct opponents for the remainder of the match, his cynical play almost daring the referee to send him off, but he remained on the field as Juventus fans celebrated a third goal from Altafini.

Juventus might well have had five goals, yet Derby came off wondering how they had conceded three. Peter Taylor and Clough – whose post match reaction was immortalised in The Damned United – were left raging, particularly after discovering Haller accompanied the referee to his dressing room at half-time. The second leg ended 0-0 and had little drama compared to that first encounter, a game often prominent in discussions of football's biggest conspiracies.

Furino and his team-mates would freeze when it mattered most, failing to make the most of the club's first appearance in the competition's showpiece event. Juventus were by this point entitled to feel confident about their chances, with the Agnelli family having constructed a truly great team. Unfortunately, the Ajax side lining up against them were a team for the ages, a side who would cement their place in history with a third straight victory in the competition. The final was the 1,000th tie in European Cup history and, after the legendary Johan Cruyff struck the post after just three minutes, Johnny Rep headed the Dutch side into the lead just two minutes later.

From then on, Ajax never relinquished control of the game, forcing Juve to become virtual spectators as their opponents demonstrated just how far ahead of the rest of Europe they now were. It was a rude awakening for the Bianconeri and Vycpálek would last just one more season, replaced first by Carlo Parola before the Giovanni Trapattoni era began in 1977. The departure of defender Sandro Salvadore a year after that poor showing against Ajax would see Furino promoted to the role of club captain and he would once again prove more than worthy of such an honour.

In much the same manner as he had made the number four shirt his own, the midfielder would appear to have been born to lead the side and it became impossible to imagine him not doing so. Beginning a unique tradition of wearing a blue armband at home and a white one away, he belongs in the rarefied air gifted to long term captains like Boniperi, Scirea and Del Piero, both in terms of longevity and importance to the club.

From the day he was named skipper until his retirement from the game in 1984, he was as vital as any other player has ever been to the Bianconeri cause. They would once again win the league in 1975 and then finish second to neighbours Torino a year later. The next season, with Trapattoni at the helm for the first time, would prove to be historic for both Juventus and Furino with the captain lifting them higher than they had ever risen before.

With just four games of the domestic campaign remaining, Juve were locked in an intense title race with il Toro that looked set to last until the very last day. They would face Napoli at a rain sodden Stadio Communale knowing a win would pile pressure on their nervous city cousins. Roberto Bettega would put the home side in the lead after fifteen minutes only for the Southern side to unexpectedly equalise through Giuseppe Massa with just ten minutes remaining.

It seemed their title bid would be spoiled by the Partenopei but Furino, as always, would never yield, floating over the mud to pick up a perfect pass from Causio and net his only goal of the season. Lazio would hold the Granata to a 0-0 draw the following day, catapulting the Bianconeri to the top of the standings and they would never relinquish their advantage.

The cushion Furino's goal gave them in Serie A allowed Trap and his players to focus fully on their UEFA Cup campaign. Having never won a continental trophy and with their failure in that 1973 encounter with Ajax still fresh in their collective memories, Juventus reached the Final to take on Athletic Bilbao, a match discussed in detail in the following chapter. The result of that game kick started the Trapattoni era in earnest and a decade of dominance ensued.

By the following season, Furino was already 33 years of age, but he was a long way from finished. The years may have passed but, despite what Brian Clough said and a string of Italy coaches believed, there was always far more to his game than merely tackling and running. Fellow midfielder Marco Tardelli called him "the most tactically intelligent player I ever saw" and as the seventies gave way to the eighties, he would begin to refine his game.

Instead of pressing on and helping the strikers, Furino would recognise that others were better equipped to do so and would fill the gaps they left behind. Displaying an incredible ability to read both the game and the intentions of his team-mates, he would cover for Tardelli's trademark runs countless times. Other occasions would see him drop into defence to cover for Gaetano Scirea as the libero strode forward to launch a counter-attack.

Without their ageing skipper, neither man would have been anywhere near as effective as they were during this time and Furino had become the glue that held those teams together. He seamlessly and selflessly linked attack and defence for Trapattoni but, as he so often did, the great Gianni Agnelli would see the captain's powers had begun to wane. The arrival of Michel Platini would effectively spell the end for the midfielder when, after speaking to the coach privately, l'Avvocato was famously quoted as saying "it is pointless having Platini if the game goes through the feet of Furino".

Massimo Bonini would gradually take over with Furino eventually retiring in the summer of 1984. The sheer statistics of his career speak for themselves: fifteen consecutive seasons and 528 appearances that see him rank third all-time behind only Del Piero and Scirea. Beyond that, he lifted eight Serie A titles, a feat no other player has bettered with the last trophy coming in his final game, as well as two Italian Cups, the historic UEFA Cup triumph of 1977 and the Cup Winners' Cup success in 1984.

Furino would never take up coaching, steadfast in his belief that nobody at the Italian school of Coverciano could teach him anything about the game he did not already know. He would return to Juventus in the early 1990s at the request of Boniperti who believed his experience could benefit the youngsters in the club's academy. He helped mould the 1994 side which tasted success both in the Primavera Scudetto and at the Viareggio Tournament, trophies following him just as they had in his playing days.

Honoured by a star on Juve's 'Walk of Fame' when the new Stadium was inaugurated in 2011, Beppe Furino may not be as famous as some of his former team-mates but his contribution to their success should never be forgotten.

THE BIRTH OF SOMETHING SPECIAL: THE 1977 UEFA CUP FINAL

Having watched on helplessly as the Ajax team cemented their legacy with their third successive European Cup win at their expense, continental competitions remained a poisoned chalice for the Bianconeri. Following on from that 1973 defeat they would endure an embarrassing run of exits from Europe, with Dynamo Dresden eliminating them in the first round the following season before a humiliating 4-1 aggregate loss to FC Twente in the semi-final of the 1975 UEFA Cup. A year later, it would be the exciting Borussia Mönchengladbach dispatching them, registering a comprehensive 4-2 win in the last sixteen of the European Cup.

The arrival of Giovanni Trapattoni would prove to be the difference maker and, as the 1976-77 season began, it would be clear that this incarnation of La Vecchia Signora was a very different proposition. The previous Serie A campaign saw them finish in second place to Torino; their neighbours not only pipping them to the title by just two points, but also ensuring they would once again compete in the UEFA Cup rather than the elite competition.

That year's draw was similarly unkind, seeing them paired with Manchester City in the opening round. Brian Kidd would net the only goal of the first leg, with the English side unlucky not to add to his strike, but Juventus would prove too strong at home as goals from Gaetano Scirea and Roberto Boninsegna saw the Bianconeri through. They could be forgiven for sensing a feeling of déjà vu in the second round, where Manchester United would also secure a 1-0 first leg lead, leaving Juve with it all to do.

By the time the second leg was played however, Trapattoni had his side playing some wonderful football and they would thoroughly outplay United, with Gordon Hill's goal at Old Trafford proving to be little more than a consolation by the time the tie was over. Two excellent strikes from Boninsegna and a third from Romeo Benetti would overwhelm Tommy Docherty's men and the same fate would befall Shakhtar Donetsk. A 3-1 aggregate win proved the Ukrainian side to be far less formidable than expected and unheralded German outfit FC Magdeburg were handed a 4-1 lesson by Juve.

That momentum would carry them comfortably through the semi-finals where AEK Athens awaited. Having been pushed all the way in their quarter-final by QPR, the Greek side were clearly fatigued and a ruthless showing from the Bianconeri saw them emerge 5-1 victors thanks to three goals from Roberto Bettega. Another final awaited and this time Trapattoni would ensure his players would not suffer from stage fright when they went up against another side yet to taste European glory.

Athletic Bilbao had completely dominated their side of the draw, helped immensely by the wave of nationalism sweeping the Basque country at that time. Just as it does today, their incredible home of San Mamés proved it is no place for visitors. FC Basel and Milan – handily despatched 4-1 in the third round – would be mere tasters of what was to come as two goals from Javier Irureta secured a draw at Camp Nou on the way to them edging out Barcelona 4-3 on aggregate.

The final would also be played over two legs, the first played at a packed Stadio Communale in Turin. The Basque side were visibly more concerned with limiting Juve's chances of scoring than getting a goal themselves and Zoff would have just one save to make, deflecting a dangerous free-kick out for a corner. They would arguably accomplish that aim more by luck than judgement as the defence, expertly marshalled by Javier Escalza and Andoni Goikoetxea, was subjected to considerable pressure throughout the game.

Juventus struggled to penetrate that back line and, perhaps worried about being caught on the counter-attack, lacked co-ordination and clarity in possession. After three minutes, Boninsegna collided with Agustín Guisasola and the striker was clearly injured, yet Trap left him on the field until just before half-time, a decision roundly criticised in the Italian press in the days that followed. Robbed of their lead striker and with Bettega isolated, the Bianconeri were relying almost exclusively of the genius of Franco Causio to create chances for them.

As he so often did when the team needed a lift, Scirea broke forward down the right and crossed towards Tardelli. The midfielder launched himself into the air, acrobatically connecting with a header that gave the home side the lead after just fourteen minutes. Yet if they thought that would see Athletic crumble, they would be sadly mistaken. Causio's mercurial left foot carved open their defence on two occasions, the first handing a golden chance to Bettega which he somehow squandered.

The second, a wonderful free kick, was met by the head of Scirea and seemed destined to double Juve's lead. Only a truly top class save from José Ángel Iribar denied them that cushion, and Juventus would struggle to trouble the goalkeeper again as time wound down. The tie remained completely balanced and after their well organised display, and it seemed the Spanish side may even have the advantage, particularly given their form at the Cathedral of San Mamés.

It would be a damp, grey evening, the Juventus mood blackened further by the vociferous 40,000 fans packed into the imposing stadium. Very few Bianconeri supporters had made the trip due to cost and the home side took full advantage in the opening moments, pinning Juve deep in their own half with both José María Lasa and Txetxu Rojo testing Zoff with well struck shots. The game quickly became a hard fought battle with Furino at its heart, as he so often was, fighting for every ball and constantly in danger of finding his name in the referee's notebook.

Then, almost from nothing, Juventus took the lead. Causio and Tardelli combined on the right wing and fired a cross into the box. Somehow, the Basque defence had lost track of Bettega, the striker finding himself completely unmarked and making no mistake with the header. It was a position, at two goals to the good, from which they would usually be expected to close out to a game, but they would fail to exploit their advantage and just five minutes later, Athletic would work their way back into the tie. Ángel María Villar delivered a perfect cross and José Churruca slotted past Zoff.

Once again, in a major final the usually confident and competent Juventus were absent as Athletic spread the play well and their wingers became a constant threat. Churruca was felled by Claudio Gentile but was denied a penalty, whilst a Dani header went narrowly over the bar with Zoff nowhere near. Vilar and Rojo tested the keeper from distance before Los Leones earned back-to-back corners. From the second, substitute Carlos Ruiz headed home and Athletic had the goal their play most certainly warranted.

With their lead now reduced to merely that of an away goal, Trapattoni's men knew what the final twelve minutes would bring. The Basque side would not disappoint, besieging the Juventus goal in search of a winner. Time almost seemed to stand still as wave after wave of attacks poured forward, forcing the nervous away side to display the qualities which many now take for granted when discussing the grand Old Lady of Italian football.

This match, this final, this last twelve minutes was almost the birth of the Juventus Spirit. The players became gladiators and the game became a test of effort and endurance, especially when entrenched in their own box as Athletic Club bombarded them with a stream of high balls and long searching passes. They distinguished themselves with a commendable performance from back to front, starting with Zoff who had often been criticised for his lack of prowess in dealing with aerial attacks but acquitted himself well here on repeated occasions.

Furino, Benetti and Gentile were their usual inexhaustible selves, while Bettega was incredible in the last thirty minutes, playing alone up front after Boninsegna was withdrawn in favour of defender Luciano Spinosi in order to protect the lead. The White Feather chased, harried and pressed the Bilbao midfield, forcing them into mistakes and truly became the first line of defence. The Basque side fought with great pride and were incredibly dynamic throughout, deserving something more than merely being runners up.

But, as good as they were, Juventus were simply better. They would not buckle, no matter what was thrown at them, simply refusing to be denied as they had in the past. The UEFA Cup was theirs, a long overdue milestone of a first European trophy that was testament as much to their physical endurance and mental focus as their undoubted technical ability. Their nerves were replaced by a steely resolve that remains evident in every triumphant side to don the famous black and white stripes ever since.

The whole competition saw them manage to overcome no less than four defeats, despite outscoring opponents by nineteen goals to seven. It had been an arduous ordeal, and it was not over yet.

Drenched by a combination of rain and sweat, the victorious players retired to the visitors' dressing room, some wearing the striped shirts of Bilbao, others drinking the sweetest Champagne of their careers. Into the celebratory atmosphere came Boniperti and, after hugging various key figures he would say something that would encapsulate everything the club legend stands for. "Now I want to win the league title at the Marassi!" he demanded, reminding the squad that there was always another game and another trophy to be secured.

The weather meant a long coach trip to Biarritz and, finally, a flight home on Agnelli's private jet. But Juventus had discovered at San Mamés that, if they worked together and refused to give up, nothing could stand in their way. Less than seventy-two hours after Furino carried the UEFA Cup down the steps at Turin's Caselle airport, the Bianconeri took to the field in Genoa and delivered the points Boniperti had ordered. A back-heeled masterpiece from Bettega and two more Boninsegna strikes delivered yet another Scudetto to La Vecchia Signora.

But 1977 will always be the year; the Bianconeri had finally succeeded in Europe, that UEFA Cup win testament to their imperious mindset and unbreakable resolve. Juventus had arrived as a force to be reckoned with both at home and abroad.

GIOVANNI TRAPATTONI & MICHEL PLATINI: THE KINGS OF ITALY

Following the breakup of the *Trio Magica*, Juventus went into a slight decline. The club looked on as the Grande Inter side became more prominent in Italy and as both they and Milan also tasted European success during the 1960s. The Milanese cousins raised the bar for Italian teams by bringing home continental trophies. While in Turin, Gianni Agnelli realised he would need something special in order to see his beloved La Vecchia Signora reach that same plateau. L'Avvocato originally believed that Heriberto Herrera could provide that, and as the Paraguayan coach added the 1966-67 Scudetto to the Italian Cup he captured two years earlier, it seemed he might have made another smart decision. It would not last, however, as after five years in Turin the abrasive nature of the 'Iron Sergeant' departed. Gallingly, he left for Inter and promptly won another title with the Nerazzurri.

As he left, an event took place that would leave an impression on Juventus for almost two decades and would continue to resonate with supporters years later. As Herrera departed to replace his namesake Helenio at Inter, the club took the decision to revolutionise the squad as the fifth-place finish in the previous campaign could not be tolerated. Antonello Cuccureddu was brought in to shore up the left flank and midfielder Romeo Benetti – so integral during the 1968-69 season – was sent to Sampdoria. That left a void in midfield which would eventually be filled by Beppe Furino, whose career spanned twenty years and is discussed in detail elsewhere.

That was all in the future however, as the Old Lady's woes were far from over. Luis Carniglia lasted just a few months as coach and Ercole Rabitti was merely a stopgap. The legendary Armando Picchi – captain of that incredible Grande Inter side – was appointed as coach for the following season, but left in February due to illness. He would pass away that May – aged just 35 – suffering from cancer, becoming the first in a line of suspiciously premature deaths of Helenio Herrera's former players.

In his place came unheralded former Czechoslovakia international Čestmír Vycpálek, a close friend of Boniperti who had given him a job in the youth sector. Promoting the striker was a gamble for the new President, but it was one that would pay handsome dividends as he led a largely unchanged squad to the Scudetto. Repeating that feat the following season was made easier by the arrival of Italy goalkeeper Dino Zoff. Already a legend thanks to his role in the Azzurri's 1968 European Championship win, he would reinforce an already impressive defence.

Wiry, and far more athletic than many keepers of the time, Zoff was rejected by both the Bianconeri and Inter as a fourteen-year old trialist due to the fact he was just 1.5 metres (five feet) tall. He would grow an astonishing 33cm over the next four years and sign for Udinese in 1961, making a disastrous debut as the Zebrette lost 5-2 against Fiorentina. He would improve over the next two seasons, moving first to Mantova and then Napoli, which catapulted him into contention for the national team. His first cap for the Azzurri came a year later in the quarter-final of the 1968 European Championship, going on to collect a winners medal as he began a journey that would see him become Italy's most capped player.

Despite losing his place to Cagliari's Enrico Albertosi for the World Cup two years later, Zoff's domestic form remained impeccable and he would move to Juventus in 1972. Both sides would never look back, the goalkeeper proving to be consistently brilliant over a remarkable 330 consecutive Serie A appearances. His ability gave huge confidence to the defenders in front of him and he always seemed to be positioned perfectly, playing with a calm demeanour that transmitted to his team mates even in the tensest moments of matches.

Yet even Zoff would still not be enough for Juventus, who fell in their first European Cup Final as Johnny Rep's goal sent the Bianconeri home disappointed once more. Vycpálek, struggling to overcome the tragic death of his son, became a part-time scout and gradually left the club a broken man. More domestic success would arrive under Carlo Parolo, himself another former player, but as the summer of 1976 approached, Boniperti, Agnelli, and Juventus were still searching for the man who would lead them to match the European feats of Milan and Inter.

Ironically, it would be a man cast aside by the Rossoneri who would finally steer them to the glory they now so badly craved. Giovanni Trapattoni – a hardnosed former player who had won all the game had to offer – was released by Milan after a brief coaching stint and the Turin giants leapt at the chance to bring him into the fold. They also gave him a squad laden with future greats, as Marco Tardelli, Claudio Gentile and Gaetano Scirea were all given their first opportunity to don the famous black and white stripes of Juventus.

What followed was the instant transformation into perhaps the club's greatest side of all time, and one of Europe's most truly incredible teams. They would march to the Scudetto with ease, setting a record as they won 51 of the sixty points available to them and finally tasting continental glory. The 1977 UEFA Cup would be a nadir for Juve as, after defeating both Manchester United and Manchester City, they reached the final against Athletic Bilbao. It was there that Bettega would write himself into the annals of Bianconeri history, scoring the vital goal as Juventus outplayed their Spanish opponents and his second-leg goal in Bilbao delivered the club's first ever victory in international competition.

That feat was even more remarkable as the team was made exclusively of Italian players, an achievement that has never been repeated. Yet for this Juventus, it was merely the beginning and they would win another Serie A title the following year. The next two seasons yielded just the 1979 Italian Cup, but the team was maturing and in both 1981 and 1982, they would win two more league titles. The latter came in a season which contained enough plot lines to make Hollywood blush and more heroes than most films produced by Tinseltown.

Paolo Rossi, suspended for his part in the 1980 match-fixing scandal had returned to Turin, eligible to play in the final three games of the season as his ban expired. Joining him were Antonio Cabrini, Massimo Bonini and Sergio Brio, adding to the quality players already present, giving Trapattoni a highly impressive squad. Going into the last match of the campaign however, the Bianconeri were level on points with Fiorentina and with both sides having relatively easy games, the stage was set for a thrilling finale.

The Viola travelled to Cagliari while Juve hosted the already relegated Cantanzaro, who were denied a penalty in the first half. Rossi was insulted incessantly by visiting fans, shouts which only intensified when the Old Lady were given a penalty for handball. Liam Brady stood over the ball, but knew as he did that Juventus had already sold him to Sampdoria despite the fact that throughout that campaign, the Irish international seemed to control the pace of every game he played. However, league rules allowed each club to own just two foreign players and Juve, who already had Polish striker Zibi Boniek, had opted to sign Michel Platini for the forthcoming season.

"There is no doubt about it, he played a really decisive role.
We might have had seven or eight players who were in the Italian
squad, but it was Brady who brought experience and personality
to the side, and his role in midfield was vital."
– Giovanni Trapattoni

Brady is said to have broken down in tears when President Boniperti informed him of the move and left many Juventini in the same state of mind. Yet, in a showing of professionalism that was becoming increasingly rare, Brady slotted the ball coolly into the corner and eternal glory was his. Except that is with Fiorentina fans, who saw him as a hate figure, while referee Maurizio Mattei, who disallowed a Viola goal that would have given them hope of winning the title race, would soon join him in that category.

A triumphant Juventus celebrated their twentieth Scudetto and the right to add a second golden star to their shirts, but the players were not done there. Zoff, Cabrini, Gentile, Scirea and Tardelli all travelled to Spain for the World Cup, a competition where Rossi would complete his transformation, from convicted cheat to iconic legend. He became top scorer in a competition Italy would ultimately win, with all six Juve men starting the final and the striker winning both the Golden Boot and the inaugural Golden Ball as the best player.

It was an astonishing reversal of fortune for the striker, who first joined Juventus as a youngster, but was besieged by knee injuries. After three separate operations, the club all but gave up on him and sent him on loan to Serie B side Como. Playing on the wing in the hope that such a role would prevent his frailties from being exposed, he rarely impressed and soon moved again, this time to Vicenza. That switch would reignite his career, as coach Giovan Battista Fabbri was forced to try him as a striker following a number of injuries. It would transform Rossi, the player displaying an incredible ability to lose his marker in the box. He would score sixty goals in 94 matches for the Lanerossi, who bid an astonishing 2.6 million lire to settle the co-ownership agreement with Juventus.

That made Rossi Italy's most expensive ever player, but in 1979 Vicenza were relegated and he would move on loan to Perugia. It was there he became involved in the Totonero betting scandal and receive a two-year ban from the sport. He always maintained his complete innocence and Azzurri coach Enzo Bearzot kept faith with the striker, taking him to the 1982 World Cup despite being in terrible physical shape. That view was confirmed in the opening matches; Rossi barely able to control or pass the ball, described by the Italian press as 'a ghost wandering aimlessly around the field'.

His fortunes would be reversed against Brazil, as Cabrini floated over a cross from the left and Rossi, as he had so many times, slipped by the defence to score with a header at the far post. He would add two more as Italy swept aside a team which, thanks to the presence of players such as Sócrates, Zico, and Falcão, came to be regarded as the finest never to win the World Cup. With two more goals in the semi-final against Poland and another in the final against West Germany, this was undoubtedly Pablito's finest hour.

He would also be named European Footballer of the Year, yet an even bigger star was on the horizon, ready to join Juve as soon as Zoff had lifted the trophy high into the Spanish sky. Having been a part of his own national team's progression to the semi-final of the same competition, no player arrived back for pre-season training more motivated than French captain, Michel Platini. Signed to replace Brady before the previous campaign ended, he and his new teammates knew that all the pieces were in place to become even greater than they already were.

Platini's impact on Juventus, Serie A and European football during his five year stay with Juventus is undeniable. Before arriving, he had inspired Nancy to a French Second Division title and a Cup win, before moving on to Saint-Étienne, France's premier club at the time, winning a Ligue 1 title during his three seasons playing for *les Verts*. He struggled to adjust in the early part of his debut season with Juventus, but eventually clicked into his best form, playing a major role the Coppa Italia win and another losing appearance in the European Cup Final. He ended the campaign as Serie A's leading scorer, and succeeded Rossi as Europe's Player of the Year with his first Balon d'Or.

It was defeat at the hands of Felix Magath's Hamburg, however, that would reignite Trap's Juve and spur them on to greater heights. Platini's sublime skill drove them on to an even better second season, as he guided La *Vecchia Signora* to *Scudetto* glory and a European Cup Winners' Cup win over Porto. Once again the league's top scorer, Platini would enjoy perhaps his greatest ever season as he captained France to glory at the 1984 European Championship. There he netted nine goals – including a 'perfect hat-trick' against Belgium – to be named top scorer in the competition and seal his second consecutive Balon d'Or.

Under the guidance of Agnelli and Boniperti, Trapattoni was able to surround his French star with a squad capable of destroying any challenger. Juve ruled Italian football, dominance built on perhaps the best defence ever assembled. The class of Zoff and Scirea was complimented by the presence of Gentile, a man whose on field demeanour could not have been more juxtaposed to his name. Born in Libya, he was given the nickname Ghadaffi and intimidated many opponents before the game even began. Scirea may have been the elegant, well-spoken ambassador of the club, but Gentile was the poster child for 1980s Italian defending with a brutal and uncompromising style which masked a superb tactical intelligence. Famously, he completely nullified Diego Maradona during Italy's meeting with Argentina at the 1982 World Cup, never allowing the captain to influence the game with a master-class of defending.

Protecting them was the tireless Furino, who did the hard work and running for Platini, perhaps the only man capable of standing up to the club's demanding President. Their most infamous exchange came when Agnelli entered the team dressing room following a win only to catch the Frenchman smoking a cigarette. Sensing l'Avvocato's concern, Platini cooly pointed at Furino and quipped "You only need to worry if HE starts smoking". Ahead of Platini were Rossi, Bettega and Zibi Boniek, the Polish striker who seemed to always deliver on the biggest occasion. As the 1985 season began, Platini was undoubtedly the best player in the world, yet there was still more to come from the man Bianconeri supporters had dubbed simply 'The King.'

———

IN MEMORIA

May 28, 1985. Like so many of us, these thirty-nine people went to watch a football match. They would never return, and will now never be forgotten.

Rocco Acerra

Bruno Balli

Alfons Bos

Giancarlo Bruschera

Andrea Casula

Giovanni Casula

Nino Cerrullo

Willy Chielens

Giuseppina Conti

Dirk Daenecky

Dionisio Fabbro

Jaques François

Eugenio Gagliano

Francesco Galli

Giancarlo Gonnelli

Alberto Guarini

Giovacchino Landini

Roberto Lorentini

Barbara Lusci

Franco Martelli

Loris Messore

Gianni Mastrolaco

Sergio Bastino Mazzino

Luciano Rocco Papaluca

Luigi Pidone

Bento Pistolato

Patrick Radcliffe

Domenico Ragazzi

Antonio Ragnanese

Claude Robert

Mario Ronchi

Domenico Russo

Tarcisio Salvi

Gianfranco Sarto

Amedeo Giuseppe Spalaore

Mario Spanu

Tarcisio Venturin

Jean Michel Walla

Claudio Zavaroni

TRIUMPH & TRAGEDY: HEYSEL & GAETANO SCIREA

"For me that cup will always be covered in death,"
– Antonio Cabrini

As Italy's most successful club, the Bianconeri have had more opportunities than most to enter Europe's most prestigious club competition and the European Cup had long been the Holy Grail for Juventus and Trapattoni. Yet, the 1984-85 season would make the club realise that you truly should be careful what you wish for.

Liverpool, led by Joe Fagan, were the continent's premier side and winners of the European Cup in four of the previous eight seasons, including a year earlier when they had beaten Roma in their own stadium. With many of Italy's World Cup winners, and the planet's best player in Michel Platini, the Turin giants were viewed as perhaps the only team capable of slowing the English club's sustained dominance.

Having lost the final two years earlier, the Bianconeri were intent on going one step further this time around, and that focus was reflected in their domestic campaign which would eventually see them finish in sixth place. Trailing eventual champions Hellas Verona by some seven points in an era where only two points were given for a win, their change in focus was all too apparent.

Thanks to their Cup Winners' Cup success the previous season, they would be given an early chance to make their intent clear in the European Super Cup. Fixture congestion meant that the game would be held as a one-off, instead of the usual two-legged affair and on January 16 Liverpool headed to Turin's Stadio Communale to face Trapattoni's men.

Much like he did against Porto six months earlier, Boniek would live up to the 'Bello di Notte' – Beauty at night – moniker bestowed upon him by Gianni Agnelli and once again shine on the biggest occasion. The Polish striker gave Juventus a first half lead and, with just over ten minutes remaining, slotted past Bruce Grobelaar a second time to hand the trophy to the home side. The Old Lady had completely outplayed the Anfield club and established herself as a genuine threat to their invincible aura.

It seemed the two clubs were destined to meet once again in the biggest game of all and, after Liverpool destroyed Greek side Panathinaikos in their semi-final, attention turned to Juve's tie against French champions Bordeaux. Fittingly it would be Platini – pitted against his French international midfield partners Alain Giresse and Jean Tigana – who dominated the two matches. His thirty-yard pass on the half hour put Boniek through to score the opening goal before another pass put away by Massimo Briaschi to double Juve's lead. Platini then scored to give Juventus a comfortable three-goal lead.

Bordeaux gave them some nervous moments in the second leg, as goals from Dieter Müller and Patrick Battiston set up a grandstand finish. If Luciano Bodini had not made a brilliant save in the last minute to deny Tigana, there would have been extra-time and Bordeaux – with the crowd and momentum behind them – would have been undeniable favourites to go through. Juventus managed to hang on, however, and set up what was immediately dubbed a dream final.

Yet the game would be little more than a footnote in the nightmare that would unfold at Heysel Stadium in Brussels on the night of 29 May 1985. Despite its status as Belgium's national stadium, the fifty-five year old ground was in a woeful state of disrepair and grass was growing through the crumbling concrete steps. Wire was all that separated the two sets of fans, while a tiny and over-worked police force fought to keep control of thousands of people using radios that had no batteries.

The outer wall of the stadium had been made of cinder block, and was literally crumbling as ticketless fans kicked holes in it to enter the arena. UEFA refused to consider a change of venue despite far better options available elsewhere, and around 60,000 supporters were believed to have crammed themselves in, despite the official capacity being much less than that. To make matters worse – and much to the annoyance of both clubs – one section behind the goal was designated as a neutral zone. Liverpool and Juventus argued this would see it filled with a dangerous mix of fans due to ticket touts and a large community of Italian immigrants living in the city.

Approximately an hour before kick-off, those fears were realised. A temporary chain-link fence was all that separated rival fans and missiles – mostly stones from beneath the terracing – were launched both ways across the divide. The tension grew as time ticked onwards towards the start of the game. A group of Liverpool supporters, scarred from their treatment in Rome twelve months earlier, moved towards the perimeter wall behind the corner flag forcing Juventus fans in the supposedly neutral Section Z to climb over the wall to escape.

Large numbers succeeded, but the wall could not withstand the weight for long and it collapsed, trapping huge numbers of people beneath it. Thirty-nine people were killed, crushed to death by the falling mass of concrete and approximately a further 600 were injured. Fans watching on television sat open-mouthed as bodies were carried away on advertising hoardings and piled up covered with flags which simply blew away as air ambulances came to help the wounded.

Juventus fans at the opposite end started fighting with police and Liverpool supporters became angry beyond reason at what they were forced to witness. UEFA ordered that the match go ahead and both captains – Phil Neal of Liverpool and Juve's Gaetano Scirea – addressed the crowd to appeal for calm before starting the game. Even as action finally got underway – some seventy minutes later than planned – riot police were still fighting a pitched battle with Bianconeri supporters.

"The players did not want to play, the authorities ordered us to. They believed that it would prevent a war between the fans but the whole evening was absolutely dreadful. And stupid. I saw bodies being taken away from the stadium. It is not good to be to playing football when people are dying around you."
– Zibi Boniek

There have always been differing accounts concerning whether the players were aware of the full horror that had occurred in the stadium that evening, but most people regarded the match itself as irrelevant. Just two minutes after kickoff, Mark Lawrenson suffered a recurrence of a shoulder injury and was replaced by Gary Gillespie. The first half passed with very few chances created at either end, but after the restart it appeared Juve were beginning to exert control over the game. It was then, after 56 minutes, the chance they were waiting for arrived.

Boniek, again relishing the big occasion, ran through the centre of the Liverpool defence and was brought down hard by Gillespie. Swiss referee André Daina – despite being left some distance behind the play – had no doubt as he awarded a penalty to Juventus. Platini stepped up to dispatch the spot kick and hand a 1–0 victory to Juventus. Some of the players, including Platini, were widely criticised for indulging in excessive celebrations given the events that had taken place, but their joy would not last.

Told of the deaths, Platini told RAI journalist Franco Costa that "faced with such tragedy, sporting festivities fade into the background. Boniperti cancelled the planned victory parade and never before or since has a European Cup win meant so little to a club, its players and fans". Speaking on the tenth anniversary of the tragedy, Platini said in an interview that the players were only partially aware of the incident. He stated that the players celebrated with the supporters in the stadium spontaneously and maintained they were all unaware of the true situation.

The Heysel disaster removed any chance of fulfillment for the players who lifted the trophy on that blackest of nights. Many more trophies and personal accolades were won by the team and its players, but their careers and lives will forever be linked with that horrific May evening in Brussels when 39 people went to a football match and never returned home.

The Bianconeri returned to domestic action with two major changes to the squad, controversially signing striker Aldo Serena from neighbours Torino while recalling Michael Laudrup from his loan spell at Lazio. To make room for the duo they sold Boniek to Roma and Paolo Rossi to Milan. Those moves, initially despised by the supporters, were soon forgotten as they made a blistering start to the campaign, winning the opening eight games thanks to six goals from Serena who ended the season with 21 goals in all competitions.

In early December, they were comfortably top of Serie A thanks to their continued excellent form which set a new record for points in the first half of the season with 26 from a possible 30 earned by Trapattoni's men. They travelled to Tokyo for the Intercontinental Cup in great spirits for what was expected to be a tough challenge against Copa Libertadores winners Argentinos Juniors. After the tragedy of Heysel, Juventus saw this game as a chance to confirm their status as the game's best team. That status would become recognised as the greatest this tournament ever saw, as both sides put on a technical and tactical display that remains unsurpassed even today.

After a hard fought 2-2 draw, the game went to a penalty shoot-out with Juventus emerging victorious as Platini scored the winning kick to make the Bianconeri the only team to have won all official international competitions available to a club side. It is an honour they hold to this day and they would soon add their 22nd league title. That title would signal the end of an era, as Trapattoni left for Inter, drawing a line under a decade of unsurpassed dominance. He delivered six league titles in those ten seasons, adding two Italian

Cups and five different international trophies, a period of success that would be almost impossible to repeat.

Rino Marchesi was brought in as coach and led them to second place in his debut season, but the inevitable breakup of the team began. Platini retired in 1987, followed a year later by the captain, Scirea, and without those two men Juventus became almost unrecognisable. If the French maestro was the attacking force that opponents feared, Scirea was the rock upon which the incredible defensive solidity of Trapattoni's Juve was built.

He is without doubt one of the greatest players in world football history and one of the only five players in European football – joining former team-mates Antonio Cabrini, Sergio Brio, Stefano Tacconi and Danny Blind of Ajax — to have won all national and international trophies for football clubs recognised by UEFA and FIFA. As we have seen, the Juventus of the 1980s was full of genuine stars with names like Bettega, Zoff, Tardelli, Platini, Brady, Boniek, Gentile and Furino, just to mention a few, but there was one above everyone else — the captain, Gaetano Scirea.

Scirea was born near Milan to Sicilian parents, he played for various local teams before receiving the chance to represent the Youth Sector of Atalanta, long considered to be one of the finest football schools on the peninsula. He would be given his Serie A debut by Giulio Corsini at just nineteen years of age, helping the Bergamaschi carve out their reputation as 'Queen of the Provinces.' Blending young talents from their successful Primavera side such as Adelio Moro and Giovanni Vavassori with the veterans who had helped them win promotion a year earlier.

Having finally shifted into the libero role after spending time both in midfield and attack, Scirea would make 58 appearances over two seasons for the Nerazzurri, playing a key role in two consecutive eleventh place finishes and Coppa Italia semi-final exits. With Juventus looking to replace their retiring club captain Sandro Salvadore, they would take advantage of their good relationship with Atalanta to bring the clearly talented defender to Turin. Scirea would be one of many Atalanta players – including iconic names such as Karl Aage Hansen and Antonio Cabrini – to be sold to the Bianconeri as Gianni Agnelli reaped the benefits of their excellent player development strategy.

He slotted into an already formidable back line – composed of Antonello Cuccureddu, Claudio Gentile, Luciano Spinosi and Francesco Morini – as though he had been there for years and would play all but two league games as the Bianconeri won the title in his debut campaign. Once ensconced with La Vecchia Signora, Scirea would mature into one of the finest players ever to grace his position and just a year later would become a regular fixture in Enzo Bearzot's national side.

By 1976, Trapattoni had arrived and he utilised Scirea's penchant for attacking as a regular feature of Juve's play. He would be a key figure as La Madama swept all before her and won a league and UEFA Cup double that sealed a place for both the club and it's most prominent defender as the continents best. Even in a land famous for producing the most complete defenders in the history of the game, Scirea stood alone in a sweeper role that has sadly become extinct in the modern age. Reading the game perfectly, perhaps only the great Franz Beckenbauer came close to the Juventus man in terms of grace, elegance, composure and intelligence.

Over the following seasons he would continue to improve. Standing as a stark contrast to the ruthless tactics often employed by others of his generation, Scirea was renowned for his class, fair play and sportsmanship. He was never sent off or suspended during his entire career, which is an amazing achievement for a defender of international level and says a lot about his temperament and skill level. He was impeccable, but a true fighter, capable of transmitting confidence and strength at the same time. Often described as a quiet leader, Dino Zoff portrayed Scirea as being "silence in a world filled with noise". So tranquil and calm was the room the two men shared on away trips with both Juventus and Italy, the rest of the squad would label it 'Switzerland'.

1982 would prove to be the pinnacle of his career for both club and country as he led Juventus to their landmark twentieth Scudetto. That win allowed the Bianconeri to add a second gold star to their famous shirts, but the captain was not done yet, heading to Spain for the World Cup. A string of unflappable performances against Argentina, Brazil, Poland and West Germany seemed to transcend the game as Italy overcame a poor start to sweep to victory. His contribution was every inch as vital as Marco Tardelli's famous trophy-clinching goal or the surprising Golden Boot explosion of Paolo Rossi. Zoff may have been the one to lifted the trophy and be immortalised across the peninsula, but nobody played a more definitive role than the great Scirea.

Four years later, Italy travelled to Mexico to defend their title but was comfortably eliminated in the second round by none other than Michel Platini and France. It was to be Scirea's final tournament as he walked away from the Azzurri at the age of just 33 to create space for younger players. Discussing the end of his journey with the Azzurri, the prestigious France Football described him as "better than Pelé, [Johan] Cruyff and [Alfredo] Di Stefano".

Two years later, having endured one of the worst seasons in Juve's illustrious history and winning no more trophies, Scirea announced he was hanging up his boots at the end of the 1987-88 campaign. He had given fourteen seasons of faithful service to the club, scaling to the very summit of domestic and European football. His list of club honours rivals those of many of the finest clubs and saw him end his career with seven Serie A titles, two Coppa Italia wins as well as lifting the European Cup, UEFA Cup, Cup Winners Cup, UEFA Super Cup and Intercontinental Cup.

He had also played for the Italian national team for more than a decade, during which he was almost irreplaceable, but gained very little recognition outside of Italy. On the evening of the Heysel Stadium tragedy it was – despite Platini being captain – Scirea who spoke on the microphone to calm the thousands of people traumatised by what was happening.

The absolute and undeniable class of Scirea is the yardstick by which all Italian defenders are judged. He was calm and Baresi-esque before Franco earned his first cap, yet that sickening night in Brussels was not the last tragedy to touch the iconic defender. Upon the end of his playing days, he was appointed assistant coach at Juve, working under his life-long friend and former roommate Zoff.

Scirea never took to coaching with any relish and embarked upon a role as a scout with the club, a job suited to lending his incredible ability to read the game into identifying potential dangers. In September 1989, he was dispatched to Poland to assess Górnik Zabrze, who had been drawn against Juventus in the first round of that season's UEFA Cup competition.

Travelling the roads at that time of year was often risky, and the car carrying him collided head-on with a truck near Babsk. The crash was made worse by canisters of petrol in the car – common practice at that time due to frequent fuel shortages in Poland – which exploded upon impact. Scirea and two of three other passengers were killed instantly, sparking an outpouring of emotion across the peninsula that very few players could illicit.

His former Azzurri coach Bearzot proposed the retirement of his number six shirt. Juventus left it unused for many years after the event, deeming it too big a task to ask anyone to follow in the great man's footsteps. His name has become attached to numerous youth tournaments and fair-play awards, citing his status as a role model for sportsmanship and sporting excellence. Juventus dedicated the Curva Sud, where the club's Ultra gathers, to his memory.

Any fan that doubts the greatness of il capitano should think of the endless list of legends who've worn the Juventus shirt. They should then realise that above all these Balon d'Or and World Cup winners, the Curva is named for our Scirea. This alone tells you all you need to know about the man known simply as the captain.

DEFINING A GENERATION:
THE 1985 INTERCONTINENTAL CUP

"I began by playing for the biggest club in the Lorraine region, went on to the biggest club in France and ended up with the biggest in the world." – Michel Platini

Liverpool and English fans were burdened with the responsibility, their hooligan element which had terrorised continental Europe over the previous decade would finally be held to account. With British Prime Minister Margaret Thatcher using the events at Heysel to press for an indefinite ban from European competition, the FA pre-empted any announcement from UEFA by withdrawing its clubs from the following season's tournaments.

Two days later the Iron Lady's wish was granted, as UEFA banned all English sides for "an indeterminate period of time". Liverpool also received an additional ban of "indeterminate plus three years", or more precisely, three further years in which Liverpool qualified for European competition. After exerting their dominance over the preceding years, as Nottingham Forest and Aston Villa joined the Anfield side in lifting the European Cup, teams would no longer be tested by England's finest.

In the days and weeks following the tragedy, Heysel would understandably continue to dominate the news. With memories of the Superga disaster, which saw the deaths of the entire 'Grande Torino' side still fresh in its collective memory, the city of Turin descended into mourning. Michel Platini was condemned from all sides for celebrating his winning goal and parading the trophy around the pitch.

"Something inside me died", he replied when asked about how he felt after realising the circumstances in which he had displayed such joy. "I didn't know that there was some problem", he continued, "I was just thinking that we could win the cup for our fans, for our city, for everybody". But that could never be, the tragedy preventing what should have been the crowning moment in the black and white shirt for Platini. Juventus had never won the European Cup and now could not celebrate the fact they had. The trophy was, as Antonio Cabrini so vividly said, "covered with death".

The Frenchman was wracked by guilt, questioning everything he believed in and wondering where he should turn. "I asked myself: 'Why do I play football?' People come to see me play and then don't go back home at all", he revealed in an interview in 2009. "It's terrible. I didn't think about retiring. My passion for the game is strong. But it was difficult". Looking for redemption and validation, he and the Bianconeri would take to the field once more, retreating to the sanctuary of the pitch and hoping that continuing to play and to win would help soothe a devastated fan base.

Having also been a part of the 'carré magique' that led France to European Championship glory the previous summer and on his way to a hat-trick of Serie A top scorers titles, Platini was, beyond question and without peer, the best player in the world. Juventus, too, were the very best, having won the league in three of the previous four years and securing four major cup wins along the way.

This was truly a team for the ages, built upon a daunting defensive unit which seemed to be impervious to any changes made by Gianni Agnelli and Giampiero Boniperti. Claudio Gentile had left for Fiorentina, but Sergio Brio, with his sleeves rolled up and his face etched in a permanent scowl, epitomised the role of the 'stopper' equally well. Gaetano Scirea was still at his peak, as he and Antonio Cabrini provided living examples of 'lo Stile Juve,' while Stefano Tacconi remains one of the most underrated goalkeepers of all time.

Massimo Bonini patrolled the centre of the pitch, tirelessly working to protect the back four and launch attacks from his role at the heart of the team. He publicly refused countless requests to play for Italy, opting instead to wait until San Marino was recognised by FIFA in 1990. The great Beppe Furino retired with more Scudetti than any other player in history. Marco Tardelli had been sold to Inter, but somehow Bonini and Massimo Mauro ensured Trapattoni's midfield never missed a beat.

Victory at Heysel should have seen the club and her fans gain deserved recognition for this truly remarkable team. Runners up in 1983, the 'Cup with the big ears' had become an obsession for this team, desperate to prove it belonged in the same breath as the other dominant sides of the era. Now that confirmation was taken from them, Platini and Giovanni Trappatoni were left still searching for that one game, that one transcendent match which would define their dominance.

The 1985-86 season would provide their zenith.

By December Juventus were runaway leaders of Serie A, having set a new points record for the opening fifteen games. They had out-scored their opponents by 25 goals to six and kept an incredible nine clean sheets. Platini was at the heart of everything, bagging nine goals while supplying a new look strike force comprised of Michael Laudrup and Aldo Serena. He had also become the first ever three-time winner of the Balon d'Or and was named World Player of the Year for the second successive season.

The club had no European Super Cup to contest, as Everton had lost the right to compete. However Juventus had secured a place in the quarter-final of the European Cup, demolishing Luxembourg champions Jeunesse Esch 9-1 on aggregate and defeating Hellas Verona 2-0. It was the Intercontinental Cup the players and supporters looked to, both to honour those lost and to truly claim their place among the greats.

Set to face Copa Libertadores holders Argentinos Juniors, the Bianconeri landed in Tokyo buoyed by their recent sparkling form, but were immediately troubled by the state of the pitch. Arriving to train at the National Olympic Stadium in Kasumigaoka, Juventus were shocked to find a surface that looked more suitable for ploughs than football players. "The ball hopped around like a rabbit", remarked Trappatoni as he feared their opponents would enjoy an advantage.

More recent editions of this competition have shown just how seriously South American teams take this competition, often playing with an intensity which catches European teams – themselves far more nonchalant towards it – by surprise. But Juve's desire to make a statement would ensure the 1985 edition was one that would long be remembered. Both teams gave their all, creating the kind of end-to-end display that is rarely witnessed in such an encounter.

Argentinos were a dangerous opponent, boasting Sergio Batista in midfield and two exceptional wingers in Carlos Ereros and José Antonio Castro. Up front, Claudio Borghi was viewed as behind only Diego Maradona in terms of skill and ability. His performance in Tokyo would tempt Silvio Berlusconi to sign him, but Serie A's restrictions on foreign players would see his career fade through a succession of ill-advised moves. But here, at just 21 years old, he would hold his team together and look to deny La Vecchia Signora the coronation she so badly needed.

Faced with such an array of attacking talent, the Bianconeri would seek to strike first, Scirea unleashing Serena, who in turn touched the ball on for Laudrup. His shot found the back of the net, only for referee Volker Roth to rule it out for offside. Almost immediately afterwards, Carlos Ereros scampered forwards and opened the scoring, executing a perfect 55th minute lob which left Tacconi as embarrassed as he was dumbfounded by the move.

The goal would see the tempo of the game increase further still, Argentinos themselves having a goal ruled out just moments later as Castro struck following some great build-up play from Borghi and Ereros. Juventus recovered quickly, their talismanic Frenchman leading them with his usual majestic touches, supplying Serena only for the striker to be fouled in the box. Platini dispatched the resultant penalty with aplomb, levelling the scores and putting Juventus back in the driving seat and he would soon have one of those truly unforgettable moments that all iconic stars have.

Pelé had his 'rounding the keeper' trick against Uruguay in 1970 and Platini matched the Brazilian here, taking three touches – never once letting the ball hit the ground – before volleying it into the net. It too was ruled out by the German referee, prompting the scorer to simply lie on the turf in defiance, his disbelief at being denied a sumptuous goal clearly visible. Sometimes a picture truly does speak a thousand words and when discussing the class, style and nonchalant grace of ease, that was Michel Platini in his pomp, the picture is unquestionably one of those images.

The following morning, la Gazzetta dello Sport would proclaim the decision 'a crime against football', but for now Juventus had greater cause for concern. Borghi seemed to feed off Platini's genius, growing in confidence and supplying another chance to Castro. The visionary pass sliced apart the usually imperious Italian defence and Tacconi was beaten once again. Juve's own number ten was not to be outdone, sending Laudrup one-on-one with Enrique Vidallé just six minutes later.

Forced to spend the previous season on loan at Lazio, the Dane had been brought in to replace Zibi Boniek and had yet to win over the supporters. Boniek was a firm fan favourite, endearing himself with a string of vital goals, most notably on big European nights. Laudrup would soon follow, rounding the keeper with tremendous skill and, despite an incredible effort to haul him to the ground, maintain his balance long enough to equalise.

The ninety minutes ended and the emotional roller coaster of the match left the players exhausted. It was no surprise that they had little to give in extra time, both coaches eschewing their earlier bravado and returning to a much more cautious style. Nothing resembling a chance was conceded and it was no surprise when it went to penalties as the two teams collapsed on the mud, each praying it would be their nerve that held. Brio opened the scoring, Jorge Olguín matching his effort before Cabrini shrugged off his spot kick miss in the 1982 World Cup Final to slot past Vidallé.

Batista stepped up next, but Tacconi guessed he would go left and parried the effort, the pain of the future Argentina coach quickly doubled as Serena extended Juve's lead. López netted and Laudrup saw a weak effort saved, only for Tacconi to once more make a save. That set the stage perfectly for Platini, who looked like the coolest man in the stadium as he strode forward for the decisive final penalty.

Staring at the keeper from just a short run up, he placed a perfect shot to the left of the goal as Vidallé dived to the opposite side and Juventus had triumphed. Finally, La Vecchia Signora had a moment to celebrate; she was the best team in world football and had proved it when it mattered most. The team celebrated long into the night and were feted as heroes upon their return to Turin, greeted by thousands at the airport as they arrived back a few days later.

Their self-belief was evident as they once again took to the field in Serie A, losing just three games all season and conceding only seventeen goals. They would lift the title, seeing off challenges from defending champions Hellas, a Diego Maradona inspired Napoli and a spirited Roma coached by Sven-Göran Eriksson. The Giallorossi pushed them hard and rumours circulated Trapattoni would be leaving after a decade in charge.

That shook Juventus deeply, but wins over Inter and Sampdoria would be enough to see them crowned champions once again. They had limped to the title but, in truth, the era had ended in Tokyo. Platini, crowned the league's top scorer in each of the previous three seasons, would add just three to his tally after returning from Japan and would retire from the game just a year later.

The Intercontinental Cup Final, a splendid match in which he had been utterly decisive, had been not only his defining moment but also his swansong. He was clearly the game's most prominent player and had proved it beyond all doubt, but this was not a match won solely for Michel Platini. This was a victory for the Old Lady of Juventus, her fans and indeed for football.

ROBERTO BAGGIO, IAN RUSH & STORIED RIVALRIES

After a decade in which Turin's Old Lady ruled over first Italian and then European football, the fall should have been expected. With Trapattoni now at Inter – who he would lead to Scudetto glory in 1989, and then the 1991 UEFA Cup – Rino Marchesi was, despite that debut second placed finish, perhaps doomed to failure. The 1987-88 season however, would prove to be the worst the club had endured in thirty years, as they lost almost as many games as they won and finished in a lowly sixth place.

The man brought in to replace Michel Platini fared even worse by comparison, as Ian Rush never reached the heights expected of a player who had netted an incredible forty goals in the previous campaign. Attracted to a move abroad by the prospect of replicating the iconic status of his countryman John Charles, much higher wages and – remembering English clubs were banned from European competition in the aftermath of Heysel – a chance to test himself against the continents best.

Arriving for a new British transfer record of £3.2 million, the Welsh striker's time in Serie A has become surrounded by misinformation and stories that bear little relation to the facts. His transfer was viewed by many as the first step in a healing process between Liverpool and Juventus, but that never truly came to fruition. While it is derided by many, Rush may have given a better account of himself had he spent more time on the peninsula. Given that many of the greatest foreign players throughout Juve's history have struggled in their debut campaigns with the club, his meager return of eight goals should have been somewhat expected.

Three of his goals would prove vital when the season came to a close, as he scored in encounters with Ascoli, Napoli and Torino to help the Bianconeri chase down and eventually catch their city rivals to force a play-off for a spot in the following year's UEFA Cup. It may not have the prestige and allure of meetings between the clubs of Rome or Milan, but for the inhabitants of the Piedmonte capital, the Turin derby is always a game of utmost importance. Like those more famous clashes, it brings joy and despair in equal measure and its heroes earn their place in the pantheon of legends for the winning side.

As with everywhere else in Italy, the hardest fought city clashes spark the kind of parochial spontaneity that unites supporters and can, in a season such as Juve's disappointing 1987-88 campaign, provide the only shred of glory in an otherwise forgettable campaign. Former Juve Chairman Alfred Dick left the club and created FC Torino in 1906, instantly creating animosity and giving birth to a rivalry which still rages today.

The Mole Antonelliana is a major landmark in Turin and is named after the architect who built it, Alessandro Antonelli. It stands tall above its surroundings with its distinctive spire every inch as synonymous with the town below as the world famous shroud now housed just a mile away. In the Italian language, the word mole literally means 'size', and is often used to denote a building of lavish proportions. As such, it is perhaps fitting that the derby encounter between the city's two clubs derives its name from the term.

Juventus and Torino contest what is known as Il Derby della Mole and, thanks to the success of both clubs, Turin became perhaps the major force in football on the peninsula. The cross-city encounter has often been seen as a symbol of the class divide during the pre-Second World War era. Juventus were closely associated with the wealthy Agnelli family, owners of car manufacturers FIAT, with Torinese novelist Mario Soldati remarking that the Bianconeri were "the team of gentlemen, industrial pioneers, Jesuits, conservatives and the wealthy bourgeois". Torino was, according to Soldati, "the team of the working class, migrant workers from the provinces or neighbouring countries, the lower middle-class and the poor".

There have also been comparisons with another northern industrial town, Manchester. Juve's widespread support across the country compares to that of United, while Torino's more localised fan base draws parallels with City. The Juventus of today may be the side in the ascendancy, but il Toro have enjoyed their own spells of dominance, particularly before the tragedy of Superga in 1949 when they were undeniably Europe's premier club.

Then, with Ferruccio Novo, the industrial magnate, as President, the club would transform their fortunes and redefine how football clubs across the globe were managed. He introduced the concept of scouting, even employing people to investigate the morale of players at other clubs as he searched for ways to bring the best talent to Torino. He did just that, bringing Valentino Mazzola from Venezia and he became perhaps the most complete Italian player ever, one of world football's truly underappreciated greats. He was a forward, a play-maker and a defensive midfielder at the same time, foreshadowing the idea of a universal player. Head and shoulders above all his peers, former team-mate Mario Rigamonti once said "He alone is half the squad, the other half is made by the rest of us together."

"He could take off like a sprinter, ran like a middle-distance racer and shot with either foot like a striker. He could leap like an acrobat, won the ball back for the defence and then set up attacks which he often finished off himself. He was both a play-maker and a match-winner." – Gianni Brera on Valentino Mazzola

Yet, despite his complete brilliance, the Granta side of that era was so much more than just their captain. Thanks to the research of Novo's scouts, other greats joined Mazzola as he built this legendary team. Men such as goalkeeper Valerio Bacigalupo, defenders like Virgilio Maroso and Aldo Ballarin joining an equally impressive midfield which blended the pace and trickery of Romeo Menti and Franco Ossola with Mazzola's all round brilliance to both protect the defence and provide the acrobatic Guglielmo Gabetto – scorer of 92 goals in 166 games for the club – with chance after chance. They did it all in a 4-2-4 formation that, over a decade later, the Brazil team of 1958 employed with such devastating effect.

They established what appears to be an unbreakable record in having all ten outfield players selected to start a single game for the Italian National team, but it would all come to a tragic end. After playing a friendly in Portugal, the team flew back into a huge storm raging across northern Italy. In unusually dense mist and fog, the pilot lost his bearings, crashing into the eighteenth century Basilica of Superga in the hills above Turin. All thirty-one passengers, including every player at the club – bar three who missed the flight due to bizarre circumstances – died instantly. Torino FC would never recover.

"Torino are no more. The team has disappeared, burnt, exploded. It died in action, like shock troops in the war. They left the trenches and never returned." – Vittorio Pozzo

They were the defining team of the 1940s, and one simply ahead of the curve in a way perhaps only seen today in the recent history of FC Barcelona. However, even their dominance pales in comparison to a group of players who to this day tower above all others in the storied history of Italian football. With robotics vastly altering FIAT's production line and the impact of the automotive industry crisis, the population of Turin fell by almost 30 percent. The total has now settled around the 800,000 mark, which is far below the level of a major city with two clubs to support. Milan for example, is home to 1.3 million people.

The success of Juventus, who won just seven of their record thirty league titles prior to the demise of their neighbours' greatest ever side, has run parallel to the demise of Torino, who have shrunk ever smaller with each passing year. Toro's ever-dwindling fan-base can never be recovered and it is not difficult to understand that those roles could be reversed had the Granata success continued unabated.

Yet during the 1970s Torino still went unbeaten over five years against their neighbours, while also overcoming them in the 1938 Italian Cup final by an aggregate score of 5-2. As their footballing stock again began to rise, Juventus were falling. The 1988 play-off would prove to be a key moment, described in the build up as 'la madre di tutte le partite' – the mother of all matches – reflecting the opportunity for adding pride to an otherwise wasted campaign. That pressure, however, led to a game where both sides were too afraid of losing to actually try to win and there was very little football played.

The inevitable penalty shoot-out ensued and, after successful kicks from Juve men Beniamino Vignola and Gigi De Agostini were cancelled out by Torino's Roberto Cravero and Giorgio Bresciani, the weight of responsibility would truly begin to show. Bianconeri stalwart Sergio Brio would see his tame effort saved by Fabrizio Lorieri, only for Antonio Comi to smash his own kick against the crossbar. The always calm Antonio Cabrini would be much cooler than he was in the 1982 World Cup Final and slotted home before Silvano Benedetti missed.

Much like Liam Brady a few years earlier, up stepped Rush to deliver the vital penalty and the high point of his brief Juventus career. He would make no mistake, wrong footing the keeper with a well taken shot and ensure the Bianconeri were in Europe the following season. The Welshman clearly suffered with homesickness, but told The Observer in February 2005 that his spell in Italy was "one of the best things I've done in my life". He was stunned to find over 5,000 fans waiting for him at the airport when he arrived and struggled to cope with the fact that only one team-mate – Michael Laudrup – spoke English. Rush spent the entire winter break in Chester and trained with his former club during that time.

"Looking back, Juventus were the right club at the wrong time," he says of the time he spent on the peninsula. "They signed seven new players and were happy to get 0-0 draws away from home. That negative approach didn't play to my strengths", and President Boniperti would decide to cut his losses, securing his return to Liverpool who happily paid £2.7 million to bring him home to Anfield. Rush never had the chance to expand on the famous line that his time in Italy "was like living in a foreign country" – that joke belongs to Kenny Dalglish – but, seeing him net just seven goals on his return to England showed his problem was not restricted to peninsula.

Marchesi also had to go, as Juve once again dipped into their vast history to find a former champion to lead them back up the table. Dino Zoff took control and was given a squad which, while losing Gaetano Scirea to retirement, would be improved by the arrival of Portuguese midfielder Rui Barros and the prolific Alessandro Altobelli. Known as 'lo Spillo', the striker would struggle much like Rush before him, but Turin's Old Lady would improve regardless of his lack of goals.

Despite never really threatening eventual champions Inter, Juve would still enjoy a memorable campaign, inspired by the tragic loss of Scirea. The team was overhauled, yet despite the many changes the World Cup-winning captain's leadership saw the side climb to a far more respectable fourth place. While being three places below where many demand the Old Lady to always sit, it must be remembered that this was achieved in a league dominated by the wealth and power Silvio Berlusconi delivered to Milan, not to mention the magical genius of Diego Maradona's Napoli. With those two clubs dominating the league, as well as transferring their superiority onto the European stage, the leap was a vast improvement.

However, it was to be in the cup competitions where Zoff's improving team would first enjoy a small taste of success. Victories in the early rounds over Cagliari, Taranto, Pescara and Sampdoria earned la Vecchia Signora a place in the final of the Coppa Italia, with the first leg in Turin on February 28, 1990. A 0-0 stalemate against the mighty Rossoneri gave real hope and belief to Juve who, until that date, had not been able to cope with the variety of weapons at the disposal of Arrigo Sacchi. Yet that confidence, as fragile as it already was, would be put on hold as the insane scheduling of the cup meant they would be forced to wait almost two whole months before the return match took place at San Siro.

Taking on il Diavolo in their own home was the most daunting experience of that period in Calcio history, as this Milan was perhaps the greatest club side of the modern era. Drilled to perfection by the obsessive Sacchi, the famous red and black shirts were worn with great distinction by iconic names such as Franco Baresi, Ruud Gullit, Frank Rijkaard and Marco Van Basten. Juve entered the second leg as the heaviest of underdogs against a team in the midst of winning back-to-back European Cups in emphatic, all-conquering fashion. It speaks to their quality that even now, over two decades later, no side has managed to match their remarkable achievement.

It is credit to Zoff's preparation that the Juventus players took the field without fear and, after just 17 minutes, Roberto Galia sprang football's most effective offside trap to hit a shot that slipped behind Milan keeper Giovanni Galli. Below the Curva occupied by his own fans, a somewhat muted celebration took place, one laced with heavy concern about the reaction of such formidable opponents. Yet as time ticked away, Juve fans dared to dream as their team controlled the match. Five long, trophy-less years – an absolute eternity for those accustomed to seeing the Old Lady forever on top of the Serie A scene – had brought a nervous tension not dissimilar to that felt over the past two seasons.

Slowly growing in confidence, Barros became a constant thorn in the side of Milan, while Sergeij Alejnikov and Giancarlo Marocchi began to dominate their more famous opponents in midfield. Pasquale Bruno and Dario Bonetti were insurmountable in defence throughout both legs as, despite Milan possessing the bigger names, the collective effort of Juventus combined to protect goalkeeper Stefano Tacconi who was excellent each and every time he was called upon. Eventually, after oh-so-long a wait, the final whistle was blown and the Bianconeri rushed to embrace coach Zoff before parading the Cup in front of their fans, the stadium emptying of Milanisti in seemingly record time.

Juventus, buoyed by finally getting their hands on some silverware, would take even greater confidence from the victory. The win had instilled the spirit back into a club that had, over five most difficult seasons, lost its very essence and, following wins over Paris Saint-Germain, Hamburg and Köln, Juventus would find themselves pitted against familiar foes in the UEFA Cup Final just over a week later. Lining up against them would be Fiorentina and despite still feeling bitterness from their 1982 Scudetto loss, events in the summer of 1990 could perhaps be cited as the genuine birthplace of this particular Calcio rivalry.

The match itself would be everything the clubs have come to feel about each other since that summer; violent, hard fought and tense, as neither side was prepared to yield to the other. Juve took a 3-1 lead in the first leg and the second leg was more of a brawl than a football match, as the game descended into chaos similar to the Torino playoff of two years earlier. The dislike grew ever greater as the Bianconeri once again ended with the trophy above their heads and just weeks later would snatch what was arguably an even greater prize.

Born in the small town of Caldogno, near Venice, Roberto Baggio began to hone his craft in the youth ranks at Vicenza, netting a simply ridiculous 110 goals in 120 matches. That staggering form would see him promoted to the first team at just fifteen years of age and he would never look back. Helping the side to a number of minor trophies including the Serie C Cup, his world would fall apart in the final game of the 1984-85 season. Playing against a Rimini side coached by none other than Arrigo Sacchi, disaster struck when Baggio attempted to tackle an opponent and suffered a serious knee injury.

He would suffer a relapse of the injury as he neared full fitness, forcing his doctors to rebuild the joint with no less than 220 stitches. Sadly it would be only the first of many similar lay-offs, as the same knee was never the same throughout the rest of his career. The inability to play the game he loved for almost two years thrust the young Roberto into a deep spiritual crisis and it was here he first turned to Buddhism. His newfound faith helped him during his recovery, but he would also be thankful that, having agreed to join Fiorentina prior to his initial injury, the Viola would honour the deal.

Taking him from Vicenza, the Pontello family who owned Fiorentina had watched the slender striker develop from a promising talent into one of Serie A's best. In his first season with the club, Fiorentina finished in fifth place and reached the semi-finals of the Coppa Italia. By this time, he was beginning to carve out a reputation as one of the peninsula's deadliest scorers. By 1989, he had attracted the attention of the entire nation and, as the Viola headed south to take on Diego Maradona's Napoli, the idol of Florence would soon become the darling of the Italian peninsula.

Collecting the ball just thirty yards from his own goal, with the sublime first touch that would typify so many of his goals, Baggio soon crossed halfway and the panic in the Partenopei defence was palpable. Looking around to assess his options, he decided to go it alone and would end it by writing the first chapter in the story of his legend. Dropping a shoulder like a slalom skier, he skipped past two defenders who came no closer to tackling him than many of the stunned fans at the Stadio San Paolo. With only the onrushing keeper to beat, he faked a shot and dragged the ball left all in one move.

Leaving the hapless Giuliano Giuliani sat on the floor behind him, Baggio passed the ball into the net with an unmatchable grace of ease.

In those ten brief seconds, a bona fide star was born. To score such a remarkable goal was one thing, but to do so while wearing a number ten shirt on the field el Diego called home saw it given even greater significance. Maradona's peak had not yet ended and he would carry Napoli to the league title that very same season, but to many observers that was the moment Baggio assumed the mantle of Serie A's most prominent and gifted player. It is often viewed as a deeply symbolic moment, and the start of the golden age of Italian playmakers with Gianfranco Zola, Roberto Mancini and Francesco Totti all joining Baggio in the coming years.

Carrying Fiorentina to that UEFA Cup Final against the Bianconeri would be his greatest achievement with la Viola and, after five years, 136 appearances and 55 goals, the Fiorentina owners decided the time had come to sell him for huge profit. Rather than watch him become the heir to legendary midfielder Giancarlo Antognoni as an idol to the supporters, the Pontellos succumbed to Juve's huge offer. To their fans however, selling Baggio – even for a world record fee – was akin to signing a pact with the devil, and when the move was confirmed, the quiet Tuscan town would quickly resemble something only Dante himself could describe. They took to the streets and rioted in protest at the loss of their favourite player, but the trouble had only just begun.

When the Italian national team headed to their base in nearby Coverciano, the crowd and furore had grown as they chanted insults at Baggio, and worse still would follow the next season when Juventus travelled to Florence for a league fixture. Gigi Maifredi had replaced Zoff over the summer, promising to deliver the 'Champagne Football' he had implemented at Bologna. With Thomas Hässler, Pierluigi Casiraghi and World Cup hero Toto Schillaci joining Baggio, hope flowed ever greater in Turin. However his tenure began in the worst possible fashion, suffering a 5-1 hammering to Maradona's Napoli in the Italian Super Cup and as the season drew to a close, they were fading badly. Juve would be dispatched from the Cup Winners' Cup in similar fashion by Barcelona, while Roma would eliminate them from the Italian Cup. With Fiorentina battling against relegation a win was vital, yet just before half-time Diego Fuser would hand the Viola the lead. Baggio's presence meant that the Bianconeri needed a police escort to the renaissance city and soon the spotlight would fall upon him once again. Just five minutes after the restart, the Bianconeri were awarded a penalty. Almost everyone in the stadium expected Baggio would dispatch it and silence the Curva Fiesole but instead he refused, leaving a stunned Gigi De Agostini with a responsibility that proved too great.

He missed, handing Juve a loss which merely continued their dire form. The increasingly peripheral Baggio was substituted less than ten minutes later and – much to the fury of the Juventini in attendance – pulled a Fiorentina scarf that had been thrown to him around his neck. The club would limp to an unacceptable seventh place and eventually Gianni Agnelli had had enough, stepping in to make a coaching appointment himself for the first time in years.

For Baggio, the story of his career in Turin would be short-lived, yet filled with incredible moments. It was with Juventus that he reached the pinnacle of his club career, inspiring the Bianconeri to recapture Serie A glory after a long drought, also lifting the Coppa Italia and UEFA Cup trophies in a five-year stay. He would become captain of a young side, collecting the FIFA World Player award in 1993 and the Balon d'Or a year later.

For the national team, he made an incredible impact at the World Cup four years earlier when he netted a goal against the Czech Republic that was eerily reminiscent of that incredible run against Napoli. But the 1994 edition of the same competition proved to be the moment which defined Baggio to a generation. Goals against Nigeria and Spain preceded a match-winning brace against Bulgaria that swept Italy into the final against Brazil. Needing an injection of painkillers prior to the game, he would take to the field with a heavily bandaged leg and failed to shine on a gruellingly hot afternoon in Pasadena.

Both teams struggled to make any impression, the first ninety minutes giving way to an equally uneventful period of extra time. For the first time ever, the global showpiece would be decided by a penalty shoot-out. Despite being clearly drained by a combination of his injury and the temperature, almost everyone watching expected him to continue his impeccable record from twelve yards. "I knew what I had to do and my concentration was perfect", he said shortly afterwards, "but I was so tired that I tried to hit the ball too hard".

It soared over the crossbar, taking the hopes and dreams of a nation with it, and that was merely the beginning of a miserable year for a devastated Baggio. Returning to domestic action with Juve, he would once again succumb to injury, this time a problem sustained in scoring another classic goal against Padova. He would miss almost six months, forced to watch on as new coach Marcello Lippi steered the team to the title with a young Alessandro Del Piero featuring in the number ten role vacated by Baggio.

Confident in the ability of his newest starlet, Lippi and Moggi decided to sell Baggio, accepting a lucrative offer from Silvio Berlusconi and Milan. Though it has since been forgotten, the Bianconeri supporters protested vehemently against the sale, unconvinced Del Piero would ever fill the void Baggio's departure would create. While time has proven that to be untrue, the transfer never really worked out for Baggio and by 1997 he was on the move once more.

Landing at Bologna, he rediscovered the joy of scoring, netting a career-high 23 goals and earning a call-up to the Azzurri for the 1998 World Cup. Despite being forced to share play-making duties with Del Piero, he would score against Austria and, thanks to penalties against both Chile and France, ensure his spot-kick woes were firmly behind him. Shortly after, he returned to the city of Milan, this time with Inter, but that too proved to be an ill-advised move. Lippi would join him there, and once again opt to use other players instead of Baggio and the Divine Ponytail made one last leap, joining minnows Brescia ahead of the 2000-01 season. Teaming up with the wise Carlo Mazzone and a young Andrea Pirlo, he would play four more years with the Rondinelle, helping them avoid relegation and recording 45 goals in 95 games.

A strong case was made for him to be part of the 2002 World Cup squad, but it proved to be a bridge too far. On May 16 2004, he would gracefully step away from the game he had made his own over the previous two decades. It was somewhat fitting that he would make his final league appearance in the grandiose surroundings of San Siro against Milan. He was substituted five minutes from time and left the field to a rousing standing ovation from all corners, the famous stadium echoing the sentiment of the entire peninsula.

Baggio is perhaps the one rare player in Italian football that transcends the petty club rivalries of Calcio, tied to no particular club and loved almost universally. That he could take up a technical role with the FIGC and be greeted with unanimous approval speaks volumes in a country wracked by conspiracy theories and partisanship in almost every aspect of life. He may not be a Juventus legend, but Roberto Baggio is a truly respected giant of Italian football.

TRAPATTONI RETURNS & MARCELLO LIPPI DELIVERS GREATNESS

It took him just seven words to get the man l'Avvocato knew would get his beloved Old Lady back on the right track. "We need a change. We need you!" was all he said, and Giovanni Trapattoni came immediately. "It was an unexpected call," the wise old tactician told Gazzetta dello Sport as he looked back on the summer of 1991, adding "I was very surprised but I jumped at the chance." Then aged 51, Trap had won a league title and UEFA Cup with Inter, but was happy to be back in Turin. Having become so accustomed to silverware arriving on a regular basis, Juventus had gone too long without a title. Watching the Silvio Berlusconi-owned AC Milan dominate the way the Bianconeri used to was getting too much to bear and Gianni Agnelli recalled the coach who had previously delivered so much.

Joining the returning Trap would be a number of players who would grow together to form the basis of a brand new side, as the remainder of his original team faded away. Having rallied under Dino Zoff for their last hurrah, those heroes of the eighties were gone and in their place came men such as Angelo Peruzzi, Antonio Conte and Jürgen Kohler. As Juve tried to overhaul the dominance of Arrigo Sacchi's Milan, the German defender would prove to be a key acquisition as during the 1988 European Championships and the World Cup of 1990, Kohler had come closer than anyone to nullifying the threat of Van Basten and Gullit.

Juventus hoped that with him in the side, perhaps they could finally challenge the previously invincible Rossoneri machine. Settling into the team, Kohler formed an excellent defensive unit with men like Ciro Ferrara, Massimo Carrera and Andrea Fortunato. In Trapattoni's first season they would come second, a vast improvement on the ill-fated Maifredi experiment and despite the distance to champions Milan, there were signs of hope.

Today, many fans of il Bianconeri have scoffed and looked down their noses at the rebranded Europa League, writing it off as vastly inferior to the Champions League and insignificant to a team of Juve's stature. While the competition is certainly bloated and ill-conceived, there is no denying the changes that its results have on the wider landscape of European football. The huge strides taken by Russian, Ukrainian, and German teams in terms of their coefficient ranking are almost exclusively due to their performances in this competition, a fact Italian teams would do well to recognise given that their indifference to it has almost certainly lost Serie A its fourth Champions League place.

The irony here is that the teams most responsible for this are those who have embarrassed themselves in the Europa League. Juventus, Sampdoria and Napoli were those in contention for the final Champions League slot that their domestic failures cost them. The Bianconeri in particular have more reason to take the competition seriously; the importance and impact it has had on the Turin clubs history simply cannot be understated. It is arguable that without the UEFA Cup two of Juve's best 'winning cycles' would have never begun, such is the belief that lifting it gave to two very different teams. In the late 1970s, a team containing players such as Gaetano Scirea, Beppe Furino, Dino Zoff and Roberto Bettega were impressive domestically, but struggling on the European stage.

Enter Giovanni Trapattoni, a renewed interest in Europe, and the club lifted its first continental trophy. Over the next eight years, they went on a unprecedented run of success, adding six *Scudetti*, two Italian Cups, a UEFA Cup Winners' Cup, Super Cup, the Intercontinental Cup (now World Club Cup) and the long awaited triumph in the European Cup at Heysel. As if once was not enough, history would repeat itself sixteen years later, in perhaps even more pointed fashion. Yet again the UEFA Cup would provide that injection of faith, as in 1992-93 Juventus would drop to fourth in the Serie A table, but would crucially win their first silverware of this new era as they claimed the UEFA Cup for a record third time.

Going into that year's two-legged final with Ottmar Hitzfeld's expensively assembled Borussia Dortmund, the two sides were deemed to be relatively equally matched despite Juve's ten goal demolition of Anorthosis Famagusta in the first round. Michael Rummenigge's early opening goal would give the German side a lead, but Andreas Möller would erase that as he inspired Juventus to serve notice to the whole continent that they should be taken seriously. His superb play created three goals as the Bianconeri stormed into an unassailable lead thanks to two strikes from Roberto Baggio and another from his namesake Dino.

The second leg would be even more straightforward, as Baggio once again orchestrated a comfortable 3-0 win for Juventus. Now the club captain, 'the divine ponytail' had become central to this new look team and was undeniably the leader on the field. It would be his best season in Turin as he scored thirty goals in all competitions, netting twenty-one times in the league to be runner-up in the Capocannoniere race. Adding six assists to that tally, his performances would see him awarded both the European Footballer of the Year and the FIFA World Player of the Year titles as the season drew to a close.

No longer the shy, diminutive figure seen in Florence, Baggio played some simply sublime football during his five years in Bianconeri, doing more than anyone to overcome the monopoly Italian football had become under Berlusconi's Milan. His touch, finesse and vision were unparalleled almost anywhere in the world and he truly was a player blessed from above. A year later, Juventus would finish second in the league behind the Rossoneri, closing the gap and strengthening the belief they could finally overhaul their rivals growing as the season went on.

Then came the 1994 World Cup and THAT penalty.

In a performance perhaps only bested by Maradona in '86, Baggio single-handedly carried Italy to the final, scoring five goals in the knockout rounds. He was openly carrying an injury as the final got underway, yet in intense heat he lasted the whole match – plus extra time – before chipping the final penalty high over the bar, handing the World Cup to Brazil. The man, who is considered Italy's most prolific penalty taker of all time, suddenly became remembered around the world for the rarest of misses.

This hurt Baggio and as he returned to Juventus, both he and the club would be unrecognisable. Clearly shaken by events in the USA, his form dipped and a power struggle developed between the player and his new coach as the summer of 1994 also saw the advent of the Triade. Composed of general manager Luciano Moggi, managing director Antonio Giraudo and new Vice-President Roberto Bettega, the three men would control of all sporting, business and financial management of the club, selecting Marcello Lippi to take over from the departing Trapattoni who had seemingly taken the side as far as he could.

The new coach had enjoyed a relatively modest time playing in the centre of Sampdoria's defence, the same club where he would embark on a far more high-profile coaching career when he hung up his boots aged just 34. Starting as a youth team coach, Lippi learned his craft during various stints in Italy's lower divisions before being handed his first head-coaching job in 1989 with Cesena. He soon moved on, first to Lucchese and Atalanta, before Moggi brought him to Napoli.

Still attempting to recover after the loss of Diego Maradona, Lippi led them to a place in the UEFA Cup, which would prove to be enough to convince the director to bring the relatively inexperienced coach with him to Turin.

Kohler, Ferrara et al provided an incredible defence in front of the superb Angelo Peruzzi, while new arrival Portuguese midfielder Paulo Sousa would be a key figure as he immediately gelled with Antonio Conte and Didier Deschamps to form a formidable trio in midfield. Ahead of them, Lippi was not convinced by the form of Baggio and turned to Alessandro Del Piero with increasing regularity, as the youngster would make 29 starts to Baggio's 17.

Yet he too was still a relatively peripheral player, as alongside him were Fabrizio Ravanelli and Gianluca Vialli, the man who would finally end Juve's longest post-war Scudetto drought. Between them, they would deliver the 23rd Scudetto to Juventus, scoring 96 goals to finish ten points ahead of the rest of the league. Having fired Sampdoria to a title in 1991, Vialli knew just what was required to end a campaign at the top of the domestic pile and Moggi believed he could make the difference for Juventus. But he was no ordinary footballer, viewed as a '*principe di calcio*' – prince of football – as his father owned a construction company and was a self-made millionaire. As a boy, the youngest of five children, Luca lived in the stunning Castello di Belgioso in Cremona, a fourteenth-century castle.

At sixteen, he would make his debut for local side Cremonese who were languishing in the third division. His impact would help the club rise to Serie A within four years and in 1984, still aged just 20, Vialli signed for Sampdoria to play alongside Roberto Mancini under Vujadin Boskov. The coach became a vital figure in his life, giving him the confidence to succeed, and the partnership with Mancini was dubbed *i gemelli del gol* – 'the goal twins' – and in their title-winning season of 1990-91, Vialli was the league's top scorer with nineteen goals in 26 appearances.

A year later the Blucerchiati, having lost the European Cup Final to Barcelona at Wembley, decided the time had come to sell their most valuable player. The supporters were devastated at the prospect of losing him and unfurled a banner at the Marassi Stadium bearing the solemn message 'sell Vialli and we will kill ourselves.' After Milan made a bid for him, the striker told a local Genovese newspaper that a move to Berlusconi's star-studded squad would be "like sticking your head in the clouds and forgetting everything that is important".

Eventually, he would agree a transfer to Turin, as Juventus paid a world record fee of fee of £12.5 million, but he would struggle with the weight that carried. His first two seasons with the Bianconeri were difficult, as a broken a bone in his foot limited him to just ten appearances in 1993-94. Due that absence, he never really found any consistency. Overcoming those problems, he would regain his best form in the following season, scoring seventeen vital league goals as Juventus pushed forward in all competitions. Netting with his right, his left, or his head, Vialli became synonymous with thumping volleys, forever changing the way Italian strikers played.

> *"If Roberto Baggio is Raphael and Alessandro Del Piero*
> *Pinturicchio, who is Gianluca Vialli? If I think for a*
> *moment I would say Michelangelo in the Sistine Chapel.*
> *He is the sculptor who knows how to become a painter."*
> *– Gianni Agnelli*

Lippi's exciting, attacking brand of football would also seal the club's ninth Italian Cup victory against Parma. Sadly Juventus lost to the same opponents in the UEFA Cup Final, narrowly missing out on a fantastic treble but marking only the second time the club had achieved a domestic double.

Once again, however, the triumph would be marked by tragedy as April of that season would see the sad passing of Andrea Fortunato, a young left back who was one of those players whose name is not instantly known to people who never saw him play. When watching your – or indeed any other – team play, sometimes a player's skill, ability, temperament or attitude reaches out and touches your heart. Certain players just connect with certain people immediately, forging a bond that lasts beyond the time at a specific club or the duration of their international career. Some are obvious; Roma fans can point to Francesco Totti, Napoli have their Diego, Milanisti have a seemingly endless list of players to choose from.

Juventus themselves can boast Dino Zoff and Michel Platini among another lengthy roll call of legends, but the club's history means far more than a list of greats. It is players like Moreno Torricelli, Alessio Tacchinardi and Angelo Di Livio who embody the famous 'Spirito Juve' that have helped make the club what it is today. Fortunato, who joined Juve in 1993 and was brilliant immediately, was one such name, as he reminded fans of Antonio Cabrini who wore the same number three shirt to such distinction during the 1980s. Fortunato's tireless running and accurate left foot provided endless crosses for the Bianconeri attack.

Arrigo Sacchi, Italy's coach at the time described him as, "the revelation of Italian football" and called for Fortunato to make his first and only international appearance against Estonia on September 22, 1993. Fortunato took Paolo Maldini's place and the side never missed the Milan man, showing just how great the newest Juve star was.

However, in a sad twist of fate, the player suffered an inexplicable loss of form. In May 1994, his doctors announced that he had a rare form of leukaemia, but he was not done yet. After a bone marrow transplant, he made a full recovery and was picked by Marcello Lippi for Juve's clash with Sampdoria on February 22, 1995. Everything seemed to be going well, until he caught pneumonia and was never able to recover. He died on April 25, 1995, on the eve of an Italy game that the Azzurri won and dedicated to him. That season's league title was also dedicated to him and is forever remembered as 'Fortunato's Scudetto.'

As important as it was, and is, to honour the defender, Juventus continued without him and, as the 1995-96 season rolled around, their one focus became blatantly obvious. Lippi's relationship with Baggio had by now completely deteriorated and he would be sold to Milan. Del Piero would benefit hugely from his departure and as Serie A finally introduced squad numbers, he would be assigned the number ten shirt that he would never relinquish. With the rest of the group largely unchanged, Italy's most successful club set about improving their record on the continent as they returned to European Cup action for the first time in a decade.

Thanks to their domestic dominance, Juventus had had more opportunities than most to enter the Europe's most prestigious club competition. Yet, their twenty-three league titles had yielded only one European Cup victory, which, at that time, was less than both Nottingham Forest and Benfica, who are hardly the most illustrious company. What also weighed heavily for the Old Lady and her fans was the manner of her previous European Cup win, as no club's first European Cup victory can ever be so overshadowed as Juve's at Heysel, where events prior to kick-off will forever be rightly remembered ahead of the victory.

"We believed you were invincible. In these 11 months you have been an example for us, for how you knew how to face real problems, not those linked to simple victories or defeats, with courage, serenity, strength and determination. We love you. We carry you in our hearts. Honour to you, brother Andrea Fortunato." – Luca Vialli

Having the tricolore on their shirts inspired this latest team and they started the season in impressive fashion. Drawn in a relatively straightforward group, they would make an early statement of intent by destroying Dortmund 3-1 at the Westfalenstadion, following that up with a 3-0 win over Steaua Bucureșt and then 4-1 and 4-0 demolitions of Scottish Champions Rangers. They comfortably won the group and celebrated by taking apart neighbours Torino in a 5-0 league win that only confirmed their superiority. Further supremacy followed the squad as the Bianconeri rallied with a 2-1 aggregate victory over Real Madrid in the Champions League quarter-finals thanks to a Del Piero free kick and a smartly taken second from Michele Padovano.

A 4-3 semi-final defeat of Nantes put the Bianconeri back in the final but, understandably, the pressure saw them finish behind Milan in the league. In the Champions League Final, Juventus would meet the reigning champions Ajax whose experience was countered by both Juve's incredible form and the fact the final would be held in Italy, at Rome's Stadio Olimpico. That historic venue would deliver a magical moment in the club's history, while simultaneously introducing a trademark celebration to a global audience. The game was only twelve minutes old when Juventus took the lead. Frank de Boer attempted to head a long ball clear, but the ball looped up in the air and left goalkeeper Edwin van der Sar stranded. Ravanelli would steal in to nip the ball away before scoring from an almost impossible angle but, on the stroke of half time, Ajax hit back. De Boer's free kick drew a good save from Peruzzi, but Jari Litmanen managed to prod the ball home and send the teams level into the break.

The second half swung backwards and forwards with both goalkeepers making a string of impressive saves as extra time became inevitable. Vialli hit the crossbar, but both sides grew nervous and the game would be decided by a penalty shoot-out. It started perfectly for Juventus as Peruzzi saved a tame first Ajax penalty from Edgar Davids. Ciro Ferrara, Gianluca Pessotto and Michele Padovano all scored for Juventus before the goalkeeper once again made a vital contribution, keeping out Sonny Silooy's spot kick. Serbian midfielder Vladimir Jugović drilled the ball low into corner and Juventus were crowned European champions.

The Olimpico erupted with joy as captain Vialli lifted the trophy high into the Roman sky, finally able to celebrate a Juventus European Cup victory untainted by tragedy. "This is for real", Roberto Bettega told reporters after the game. "We could never celebrate winning in

1985 and have waited a long time for this". But today when a player pulls his shirt over his head to celebrate a goal, Italians – rather than lament the over-officious nature of the rule that sees the scorer receive a yellow card – are taken to an event that left an indelible mark the conscience, as the act sparks a nostalgic trip down memory lane.

Born in Perugia, where Fabrizio Ravanelli would both begin and end his career, la Penna Bianca – 'The White Feather' – was a classic striker with a deadly left foot and good in the air. He eventually developed the instincts of a genuine predator. Trapattoni was still the coach when the player was brought to Turin and his raw talent was honed by the veteran tactician who worked closely with him to ensure he realised his vast potential. His first season saw him being largely an underused reserve behind Pierluigi Casiraghi, Vialli and of course Baggio, but this allowed him to improve his game with much less pressure and his mentor's faith would be repaid in time.

During the 1993-94 season, Ravanelli played a small role in one of the club's most historic occasions when Trapattoni substituted him in the 80th minute of a match against Reggiana. His 18 year-old replacement came on to score his first goal for the club, thus starting the legend of Alessandro Del Piero. Ravanelli also became more of a regular that season, and was clearly happy to be at the club.

"To have arrived at Juventus is the best, I feel I've become a man and made it as a player. Juventus is the maximum and those who speak evil of us do so only out of envy. I hope people comparing me to Bettega don't do so just because of our hair."
– Fabrizio Ravanelli

In the 1994-95 season, Lippi pushed him firmly into the limelight, and once there he shone, reaching the height of his career. He made a major contribution to winning the Scudetto as his fifteen goals were second only to Vialli, and in the Italian Cup he scored in the final as Juventus beat Parma. In September of 1994, Ravanelli blew the whole of Europe away with a 5-goal performance – still a record to this day – in Juve's 5-1 UEFA Cup win over CSKA Sofia. His fine form continued in the following campaign and in the Champions League Final he would once again deliver when it mattered most.

The season was a remarkable one for the striker and he contributed with some vital goals, but none more so than that cut-back from the narrowest of angles against Ajax. It all comes back to that goal; the high bouncing ball, a touch to take him away from Van der Sar, the instinctive finish and he's off running down the touchline, Vialli in pursuit as he once again shows off that signature celebration.

That summer, Moggi would do what many others have failed to do and shook a winning team to its very core. Vialli, tired of arguing with the club over a new contract, left for Chelsea and Ravanelli would be sold to Middlesbrough. Pietro Vierchowod, Massimo Carrera and Paulo Sousa all left, replaced by Zinedine Zidane, Alen Bokšić and a young Christian Vieri. The campaign would see Del Piero enjoy perhaps his best solo season as the club celebrated its centenary year in spectacular fashion. In November of 1996, Juventus headed to Tokyo and won the Interconinental Cup for the second time in their history.

They added the European Super Cup courtesy of a 9-2 aggregate win over Paris Saint-Germain in January, and at home there was an incredible 6-1 win over Baggio and Milan at San Siro as Juventus once again tasted Scudetto champagne. The defence of their Champions League title was punctuated with two wins over Manchester United, while they eliminated Ajax in the semi-final to enter the final match against old foes Borussia Dortmund. Lining up against them were three of the men who had helped the Bianconeri win the 1993 UEFA Cup – Kohler, Möller and Júlio César – but unlike the previous season, they would be the visitors as the game was played in Munich.

Juventus came into the game as strong favourites, a testament to both their status as holders and their form that season. They started brightly and had Vieri showed better poise in front of goal, the game may have been over before it reached half-time. But he didn't, and Juve's usually well-organised defence was stunned by a stellar display from Karl-Heinz Riedle. He scored two goals from corners, first cushioning Paul Lambert's cross on his chest and firing a shot under Angelo Peruzzi, before striking again with a powerful header.

Lippi's men responded well; first hitting the post with a great Zindane effort, then Vieri struck the bar with a deflected effort before also having a goal disallowed. Del Piero was introduced at the interval and would brilliantly flick home Alen Bokšić's cross to give them some hope. Minutes later, that hope turned to despair as substitute Lars Ricken broke and chipped past Peruzzi from some distance to ensure victory for the German side. He had only been on the field for sixteen seconds, but that was all it took for Dortmund to gain their revenge for that 6-1 demolition in the 1993 UEFA Cup Final. Coach Ottmar Hitzfeld was stunned by his side's win, telling reporters at the post-match press conference that the game "was a big surprise" because "Juve had great players and were unbeaten in two years".

Moggi would again react, shipping out Attilio Lombardo, Jugović, Bokšić and Christian Vieri, hoping to pair Del Piero with a 23-year old Filippo Inzaghi, who had been named both Serie A's Best Young Player award and top scorer the season before his arrival. The two men could not be more different. Del Piero a classy, dignified one-club legend that receives world-wide admiration and respect and Inzaghi, the infuriating, unloved, often criticised poacher who was – to quote the great Sir Alex Ferguson – 'born offside'. For four years at Juventus the two men were team-mates, although perhaps that term is a stretch given the fractious relationship between the pair. The partnership was deemed to be too lightweight from the start, and doubts about their ability to play together were widely held.

As has since become a trademark of both men's respective careers, they would make nonsense of this criticism, inspiring the team to another league title and a place in their third consecutive Champions League Final. Inzaghi netted eighteen goals in Serie A and six more in Europe, while Del Piero had arguably the best season of his career with 21 league goals. The latter would also end the season as Champions League top scorer with ten.

The title would not be without controversy, however. Most notably in an April 1998 meeting with title rivals Inter, with Gigi Simoni's side arriving at the Delle Alpi trailing Juve by just a single point. They were carried by £24 million signing Ronaldo, who was terrorising opposing defenses on his way to scoring 34 goals in his debut campaign with the Nerazzurri. A win could spur them on to their first title in a decade, but the events which unfolded that day would last even longer in the memory of Calcio fans everywhere.

Del Piero opening the scoring in the 21st minute but, as Ivan Zamorano passed to Ronaldo, it would be referee Piero Ceccarini who would take centre stage. Mark Iuliano lent into the Brazilian as he flicked the ball on, appearing to obstruct his progress but the official waved play on. Inter players and coach Simoni were furious and those feelings would only intensify as Del Piero raced up the pitch and was pushed by defender Taribo West. This time Ceccarini pointed to the spot and Inter players surrounded the referee and remonstrated at length, with Simoni eventually being sent off. Gianluca Pagliuca would save Del Piero's resultant penalty, but the game finished 1-0 and the Bianconeri went on to lift the Scudetto once more.

In an interview years later, Ceccarini said he "didn't see Iuliano" and believed Ronaldo had simply run into Iuliano and fallen over. He conceded after seeing replays of the event that he should have given an indirect free kick for obstruction, rather than a penalty but the debate raged in the press for months. A few days after the game, there was an actual fight in parliament during a publicly broadcast session, as Domenico Gramazio of the National Alliance yelled "You are all thieves!" at fellow politician and former Juve midfielder Massimo Mauro. The session was suspended with Deputy Prime Minister Walter Veltroni telling the warring duo "We are not at a stadium. This is a spectacle that is unworthy, embarrassing and grotesque!"

Back in Europe, the Bianconeri dispatched Monaco 6-4 on aggregate in the semi-final, with Del Piero – who would be the tournament's top scorer that season – putting on a sublime display. A hat-trick in the first leg at home included what was arguably the best free kick of his career past Fabien Barthez. That was followed up by a stunning volley in the second leg as the Bianconeri reached their third consecutive final. Lippi described meeting Real Madrid at the Amsterdam ArenA as the 'dream final', but sadly it would not turn out that way as a season which should have been one of the best in their history quickly became the start of a nightmare.

While Juve were still regarded as the best team in Europe, their Spanish opponents were in poor form having been eliminated from the Copa del Rey by a third division side and finishing fourth in La Liga. Dominating the first half, the Bianconeri were expected to win easily. Zidane came closest to finding the net, with Mark Iuliano and Edgar Davids having great chances to open the scoring. Predrag Mijatovic – who had appeals for a penalty turned down early in the game – then pounced to score the only goal of the game in the 66th minute.

There was a huge amount of fortune to the goal, as a Roberto Carlos cross deflected off Iuliano. However, the striker's first touch was superb and he rounded Peruzzi to net, despite Juve's appeals for offside. From there, Real Madrid defended superbly, with Fernando Hierro in particular making up for the way Del Piero had previously embarrassed him. Coach Jupp Heynckes was sacked regardless of the win, with President Lorenzo Sanz claiming "if we hadn't won that title, this would have been one of the worst seasons in our history".

After a season of proving their doubters wrong, Del Piero and Inzaghi had seemingly become Italy's most deadly of duos, but their troubles were about to come to a head as 1998-99 began. First came that fateful game in November 1998 away in Udine as Del Piero collapsed to the turf with nobody near him. Instantly knowing something was wrong, hearts were in mouths as he was carried from the pitch.

He took Juve's hopes with him as they added a heartbreaking Champions League elimination to eventual winners Manchester United, to a disappointing seventh place finish in Serie A.

Injured and out of the team for over a year, when Del Piero returned it was to a very different Juventus. Marcello Lippi was gone, sacked in February, and replaced by new coach Carlo Ancelotti. It seems hard to believe now, given his successes at Milan, Chelsea and Real Madrid, but the arrival of the former Azzurri midfielder was very badly received in Turin. Dubious about the ability of their new boss, Juventus fans unveiled a banner reading 'a pig can't coach' in reference to Ancelotti's farming background. His tenure did not begin well despite Moggi pleading with the supporters to back him, the director clearly able to see his ability.

But the team was already out of both the title race and Champions League, eventually gaining entry to Europe via the Intertoto Cup, entry to which was only earned via a play-off against Udinese. In the absence of Del Piero Inzaghi had thrived, scoring twenty goals and carrying the team at times. He had become an important element in the team, firing them to success in both the playoff and the subsequent Intertoto campaign.

Del Piero struggled upon his return, not finding the net from open play, but the club backed him fully, allowing room to recover. Ancelotti selected him constantly in an attempt to help him regain that magic touch. The team was very different too, with Van der Sar, Edgar Davids and Gianluca Zambrotta arriving to replace his close friends Angelo Di Livio, Peruzzi and Deschamps. Perhaps it was here the differences between Del Piero and Inzaghi truly began, with jealousy on both sides preventing the renewal of a proven partnership.

The season began brilliantly and Juventus led the league for most of the campaign, losing just one of their first 26 matches, but the success would not last. Despite going into April with a nine-point advantage, they collapsed over the final eight games, losing four matches including a key meeting with title-chasing Lazio. During this time, the football world paid even closer attention to Inzaghi and Del Piero with each shot, gesture and glance analysed in slow motion to find out the feelings of the two men. The captain seen raising his arms in desperation as he waited for a pass that would never arrive from Inzaghi became an all-too-familiar sight and seeing them this way in the flood at Perguia on the season's final day perfectly summed up their relationship at that point.

The Bianconeri travelled there and, despite their poor form, were expected to seal the title. In Rome meanwhile, Lazio – the only side who could prevent Ancelotti's men being named champions – would take on Reggina at the Stadio Olimpico. The venue for Juve should have provided a warning, as it was also where, twenty-four years earlier, a Renato Curi goal denied them the title on the last day. The stadium had been named after Curi following his death on the field there in 1977, the midfielder suffering a heart attack during another game against the Bianconeri.

If that went unheeded, nature would seem to conspire against the visitors. Having kicked off under bright blue skies, rain, hailstones and a thunderstorm hit the Umbrian town, as the rest of the country enjoyed late spring sunshine. Lazio's performance was given a huge boost after they were awarded two penalties and while the first was indisputable, the second was dubious to say the least. Simone Inzaghi rolled in the first following a clear handball, but when Giuseppe Pancaro came forward from his full-back position, a slight pull on his shirt sleeve saw him take a theatrical fall and the referee again pointed to the spot. Juan Sebastián Verón scored the resultant spot kick but Juve's anger toward match officials was only just beginning.

The deluge in Perugia had left the pitch waterlogged and forced referee Pierluigi Collina to delay the start of the second half by almost ninety minutes. Diego Simeone made it 3-0 for Lazio as their fans were celebrating, looking on as Roberto Mancini called time on his eighteen-year career. The striker danced around the perimeter track, as the Lazio match, and all others in Serie A, finished even before the second half in Perugia could commence. Umbrella in hand, the most famous of officials went out onto the pitch with the two captains, farcically throwing the ball into the air, only to see it sit in a puddle and cease to bounce. Yet he refused to call off the match and restarted the game, despite the playing surface becoming a rain-sodden hazard.

Alessandro Calori would give the home side a shock lead; the big defender was lurking inside the penalty area four minutes into the second half when the ball broke his way. He showed incredible ability to control the ball with his chest before looking every inch the world class striker, as he dispatched the ball past Van der Sar with his right foot. The Biancocelesti half of the Italian capital rejoiced even as Collina prolonged the Juventus agony for five minutes of injury time.

Lazio would be champions for only the second time in their history by just a single point, the rain helping to settle the most dramatic and suspicious of all Italian seasons. But the game gave credence to the urban legend that Del Piero and Inzaghi never passed to each other and, truthfully, there is plenty of evidence to back up those claims. What quickly became clear the following season was that the newly arrived David Trezeguet was a far better fit alongside Del Piero and Inzaghi, much like Ancelotti, would not remain in Turin much longer.

———

MAY 5 2002: THE BIRTH OF A NEW RIVALRY

"I hope Juventus win 10-0. The truth is Inter don't know how to lose & start crying" – Luciano Moggi

Just as they had the season before, Carlo Ancelotti's Juventus would end the 2000-01 season in second place to a club from Italy's capital city. Unlike the previous season, there would be no controversy even as they again took the title race to the final day, this time losing out to a highly impressive Roma side led by Francesco Totti, Gabriel Batistuta and coached perfectly by Fabio Capello. Juventus would simply not settle for a runners-up spot and, much as they had when looking to end their title drought a decade earlier, they turned to the man who had previously delivered silverware with incredible regularity.

With echoes of Trapattoni, Marcello Lippi too had left Turin for Inter, where he was unceremoniously fired on the first day of the previous season at a time when the whimsical nature of Massimo Moratti was at its fullest. The club he had left behind once again invested millions to build a talent-laden team to support the seemingly dream front pairing of Christian Vieri and Ronaldo. With Álvaro Recoba and Sérgio Conceição in attack and Marco Materazzi protecting goalkeeper Francesco Toldo, new coach Héctor Cúper had all the tools at his disposal to end the Nerazzurri's thirteen-year wait for lo Scudetto.

Luciano Moggi would provide Juventus with a surprising summer, not only reappointing Lippi but also selling Zinedine Zidane to Real Madrid for a world record fee. With Filippo Inzaghi moving to Milan and Fulham snapping up Edwin Van der Sar, the Director General had more money than ever to reinvest in the squad as he sought to return La Madama to the very top of Italian football.

In order to make clear that they intended to end Rome's dominance of Serie A before it could truly begin, the Bianconeri would secure the signatures of French defender Lilian Thuram and Lazio's talismanic midfielder Pavel Nedvěd. Their spending would catch global attention as they handed Parma no less than €45 million to bring Italy's premier goalkeeper, Gianluigi Buffon, to the club in a deal which was far from easy to complete.

Initially swayed by his friendships with Francesco Totti and Vito Scala, Buffon's father and agent travelled to speak to the Roma President Franco Sensi, only to discover the capital club were looking to spend less. The Giallorossi opted instead for Ivan Pelizzoli and the player's representative Silvano Martino would then head to Spain to conclude a deal with Barcelona, the Catalan giants keen to bring Buffon to Camp Nou.

"Then Moggi and the Agnelli family stepped in", Buffon would remark years later. "I really wanted to win a Scudetto, my father said Juve hadn't won the title for five years and that they were bound to win it within the next two years". Heeding his advice led the son to enjoy great success, but his early days in Turin were a far cry from the dominant displays normally associated with Italy's undisputed number one.

The 2001-02 season began well for the Bianconeri and Buffon, routine wins over Venezia and Atalanta coming with two clean sheets for the record signing and proof that David Trezeguet was indeed the perfect foil for Alessandro Del Piero. With both now assured of their places, they each had netted three times in those opening two victories and it seemed the sweeping changes had indeed brought about an upturn in fortune.

It was then that the first problems began, a week three encounter with newly promoted Chievo bringing the first questions of Buffon's ability to cope with the twin pressures of Juventus and that huge transfer fee. Coming to claim a simple high ball at a corner, he would somehow catch the ball, but then gift it at the feet of visiting striker Massimo Marazzina who gave the minnows a surprising 1-0 lead. He would double the advantage ten minutes later and the new look Bianconeri suddenly had a game on their hands in the most unexpected circumstances.

With Lippi on the bench however, Juventus would react as she always has when faced with such adversity, launching a furious comeback as if they already knew what would be written in the next morning's press should they fail. Alessio Tacchinardi would reduce the deficit and what followed was an onslaught of attacking football; a disallowed Trezeguet effort one of countless attempts at drawing level, with Igor Tudor eventually restoring parity just before half-time. Then, seven minutes from the final whistle, substitute Marcelo Salas would net his first goal for the club from the penalty spot, earning Juve a victory which had looked unlikely only an hour earlier.

Buffon was lambasted for his mistake, one he would compound with further errors against Hellas Verona and in the derby against Torino, and the sum Juventus had invested in him began to look as if it would backfire spectacularly. Steadily however, as the reconfigured side in front of him learned to play as a more cohesive unit, the goalkeeper's previously excellent form would be rediscovered and the Bianconeri would climb the table and present Inter with a stern test of their championship credentials.

With reigning champions Roma also contesting things at the top of Serie A table, the three giant clubs would match each other all the way, trading blows from the mid-point of the campaign until the very end. The Giallorossi lost narrowly to Juventus in Rome, despite the visitors seeing Mark Iuliano receive a first half red card. Inter and the Bianconeri would draw in Milan on the same weekend as a four goal haul from Vincenzo Montella inspiring Fabio Capello's men to a 5-1 derby victory over Lazio. With five games remaining, Juve would drop vital points to fall six points behind the lead, only for Atalanta to record a famous win away to Inter which prompted *Corriere dello Sport* to declare that the Nerazzurri were "running scared" in their bid for the championship.

The biggest controversy would come in Roma's late draw at Venezia in Round 30, with Montella scoring a goal which may well have been disallowed and notable referee Pierluigi Collina was banned from taking charge of any of the title challengers remaining fixtures after awarding the Giallorossi two late penalties. Juve would win four straight matches – a run which including a last-gasp Nedvěd winner at Piacenza – to bring themselves back into contention. Once again, the last round of the league would begin with the teams at the top separated by two points, Inter entering Round 34 with 69, Juve narrowly trailing on 68 and Roma a further point back in third place.

All three had away games on a last day, which would become one of the most famous in history and – on paper at least – it appeared Inter would have the most difficult task as they would line up against Lazio, themselves champions just two years earlier and still in contention for a European place. As kick-off drew near however, the home supporters were clearly hoping their side would lose to ensure Roma could not pass the Nerazzurri and secure a second straight title. Much of the stadium was decked in Inter colours, making it feel more like a home game for the Milanese visitors.

Roma themselves were facing a Torino side with nothing to play for and would also hope not to hand the title to their own derby rivals, while the Bianconeri were pitted against Udinese. That meant Del Piero and his team-mates would take the field at the Stadio Friuli hoping the number ten could exorcise his personal demons of the 1998 injury at the same stadium and lead them to glory.

As the matches began simultaneously on the sunny afternoon of May 5, the conditions were perfect for football and the huge contingent of travelling Juventus supporters would not wait long for their side to strike the first blow. With both the Bianconeri and Roma reliant on results going their way, Capello's pre-match opinion that "all three will win and the table will not change" would look as though it would be proven correct. With just 68 seconds on the clock, Trezeguet would net the first goal of the round as he headed home a cross from Antonio Conte and, just ten minutes later, Del Piero would double their lead.

The captain finished off a swift Bianconeri counter attack with a cool finish and, as they set about protecting their early lead, thoughts turned to events in Rome. Inter fans had travelled there in droves too, hoping the hurt and anguish they had endured since their previous triumph – back in 1989 – would finally be over. Despite Lazio goalkeeper Angelo Peruzzi handing Vieri the simplest of chances to open the scoring, with a mistake echoing Buffon's from earlier in the season, the opening 45 minutes would prove to be another roller-coaster of emotions for those of a Nerazzurri persuasion.

From the very first minute, Lazio fans had let their feelings be known, booing their own players whenever they touched the ball and cheering Inter as they went into the lead. "It was surreal, I've never known anything like it", said shaken Lazio player Stefano Fiore after the game. It would become an even stranger atmosphere when former Manchester United winger Karel Poborsky made it 1-1, but then a Luigi Di Biagio header from a corner would restore the visitor's lead.

Then, just before half time, Dejan Stanković – who would go on to enjoy a fine career with Inter – would hit a cross from the right which was headed away by Iván Córdoba. The danger seemed to have passed, only for everyone who held the Nerazzurri dear to look on helplessly as Vratislav Greško made himself the club's least popular player in decades. Inexplicably, the Slovakian – who would never again wear the black and blue striped shirt – chose to try to head the ball back to Toldo instead of making a simple clearance. Poborsky would pounce once again, slotting past the stranded goalkeeper and ensure Juventus would head into half-time with one hand on the title. An eerie silence descended over the packed Stadio Olimpico, 80,000 people completely unsure of how to voice the feelings the tumultuous match was evoking.

Having suffered through two consecutive final-day heartaches in each of the previous two seasons, the Bianconeri would be taking nothing for granted. As the second period in each match got underway, all eyes would be looking to see how a visibly shaken Inter would respond. They began a hectic hunt for goals that would end their own decade of torment, but instead it would be another of their own future players who would extend their pain. Diego Simeone would join the Nerazzurri a year later, but here he would catapult Lazio into the lead, with the Rome club's fans finally celebrating, safe in the knowledge their own bitter rivals would not end the day triumphantly.

Giuseppe Favalli – yet another player who would later move to Inter – almost netted an own goal, prompting a chain-smoking Héctor Cúper to bring on Stéphane Dalmat in place of Conceição as their quest for goals continued. Elsewhere, Cassano gave Roma the lead and his superb chipped effort pushed Inter down to third place with just twenty minutes of the season remaining. Minutes later, a Simone Inzaghi header made it 4-2 to Lazio and Mohammed Kallon was sent on in place of the ineffective Ronaldo as Inter's tension turned into pure panic.

The goals never came and, with time ticking down, it became abundantly clear that the Inter dream was over for another year. Ronaldo, sitting on the bench, broke down in tears, the pain and disbelief of what had transpired that afternoon simply too much for the Brazilian to take. In the stands, Massimo Moratti was stunned and on the field Marco Materazzi was incredulous. "I helped you win a title!" he shrieked at opposing players, a clear reference to his stint at Perugia two seasons earlier, the defender having played a major part in their victory over the Old Lady which handed Lazio the Scudetto.

Somehow, inexplicably – and in the most unbelievable circumstances – Juventus had won a title and ended their run of horrific bad luck which began that day in the torrential Umbrian rain. Marcello Lippi had once again taken La Madama by the hand and guided her to instant success, the coach further cementing his place in both the hearts of Bianconeri supporters and in the pages of club history. Discussing his four league titles with the club as he left the pitch, he would tell reporters that "they were all great feelings, but this one is the strongest".

While Ronaldo would soon be happy in Madrid – the staggering loss proving to be his last appearance for Inter – a feud began between Antonio Conte and Materazzi that still rages today. "This is for the disappointment of two years ago at Perugia and there is someone watching who was at Perugia..." screamed Conte to reporters at the final whistle. His voice laden was with emotion and vitriol for a man whose actions had so angered everyone connected with the Bianconeri. "There you were laughing at us", the veteran midfielder raged, "today you are crying...I am so happy!"

Full of vengeance, the Juventus captain was angry with the defender for "lacking respect" during that rain-drenched loss two years earlier. Materazzi responded, telling Conte to "buy himself a new wig with his championship bonus!" Determined to have the last word, Conte would say "nobody uses wigs anymore but you can have a hair transplant. Unfortunately for him, brain transplants still don't exist!" Their spat often resurfaces even today, as do pictures of Ronaldo's tears on the day the bitterness was put into the Derby d'Italia.

The Juventus rivalry with Inter was so named, like many things in Italian football, by the great Gianni Brera, the famous Italian journalist coining the phrase in recognition of the two most successful teams in the country during his writing career. Events in 2006 ensured it would become even more vitriolic and combustible, but this rivalry is one littered with scandal, intrigue and bad behaviour and it began long before Brera even bestowed the famous moniker upon it.

Its origins lay in that 1960-61 abandoned match, eventually awarded as a win to Inter after a pitch invasion in Turin. After appealing to the Italian football association, Juventus secured a replay and a disgusted Nerazzurri responded by playing their youth team. Juve went on to record the fixture's most one-sided result as Omar Sivori scored six goals in a 9-1 thrashing, which secured not only the league title, but also the top-scorer crown for the Argentinian who won that year's Ballon d'Or.

The next two decades were a quiet period for the derby, as Inter continually failed to reach their previous greatness; until that incident-filled encounter in 1998 re-ignited the old hatred and bile. That April was the scene of the previously discussed Mark Iuliano-Ronaldo penalty call which led to a session of Italian Parliament actually being abandoned, as deputies from the far-right National Alliance and Democratic Left came to blows over accusations of match-fixing. The 20 seconds between the body-check and the award of a penalty to Juve became among the most replayed in history; countless television programmes slowing them down and discussing them.

Since that day, which became known as "The Grand Thievery" to Inter supporters, it has grown to become easily the most intense inter-city rivalry in the country. Two years after the Ronaldo incident, Paolo Montero was banned for punching Inter midfielder Luigi di Biagio in the ear and then the events of the Calciopoli scandal – and each side's view of the other's role in it – escalated the hate and vitriol to a now ridiculous level.

The title win on May 5, 2002 will perpetually mark the day meetings with Inter took on new meaning as the rivalry resonates every season with the imagery and memories of that fateful spring afternoon. Juventus fans will treasure them forever.

———

THE END OF LIPPI BRINGS FABIO CAPELLO BACK

If the unlikely title win in 2002 drew the clearest ever picture of Inter's weaknesses, it certainly highlighted the mental toughness of a Marcello Lippi-led Juventus. It was achieved by a side filled with players who, much like Giovanni Trapattoni's great teams, would simply never give up. While packed with quality, these incarnations of the Bianconeri were never truly as talented as the squads built by Massimo Moratti and Silvio Berlusconi's millions, but they had intangible qualities money simply could not buy. The effect of the two legendary Juventus coaches was monumental and it is still impossible to look at their triumphs and not acknowledge the impact Luciano Moggi's arrival had had on the club.

The director, who had first come to prominence in Naples, was always a shadowy figure. His methods in becoming the greatest power-broker in the modern era were questionable from the beginning but, in such a results-based industry as football, nobody would argue with the achievements of the Tuscany native. He might not have possessed the famous 'Juventus Style', but he was incredible at spotting players who did and the list of deals he made has unsurpassed by any other sporting director.

The summer of 2001 notwithstanding, Moggi rarely bought the finished article, plucking players either from obscure locations or the bottom of the scrapheap. He notably resurrected the careers of players such as Edgar Davids and Fabio Cannavaro when others in Italy believed they were finished. The summer of 2002 saw him operate on those lines once again as he brought Mauro Camoranesi from Hellas Verona, thrusting him into the limelight at one of Italy's biggest clubs.

"He was not just interested in the ability of a player but in his family situation, in his personality. He was not just a manager but became a second father, an older brother and was very successful as a result." – Marco Travaglio, Il Giornale

Juventus began the following season in superb fashion, lifting the Italian Super Cup by defeating Parma in Tripoli thanks to two goals from Alessandro Del Piero. The team followed that up with a 4-0 win over Torino and a 3-0 victory over Inter. However, the season would be rocked when, on January 24, the man so beloved by all those of a Bianconeri persuasion passed away. After a long battle with cancer, Gianni Agnelli sadly died. Two days later, Del Piero would net against Piacenza and his goal was dedicated to the man behind so much of Juve's success. "Today it is a special day," Del Piero told reporters, "we tried to do our best. We had played a good first half and wanted to send him our message, we hope we have done it."

It would be in Europe where they would once again look to leave their mark. Comfortably through the first group stage of the Champions League, it would take a superb Igor Tudor strike against Deportivo La Coruña to confirm qualification from a second pool, which also contained Manchester United and Basel. That put them into the quarter-finals where Barcelona awaited and, after two difficult legs, the tie was level at 2-2 with the Bianconeri seemingly heading out on away goals. Down to ten men, Juventus were forced to soak up endless Barcelona attacks as Patrick Kluivert and Luis Enrique had glorious chances to win, but Buffon was equal to everything the Catalan side had. With just five minutes remaining, and in virtually their only attack of the extra period, Marcelo Zalayeta connected with a cross to keep the dream alive.

In the next round, it would be the Galactico-era Real Madrid standing between them and a place in the final. Laden with familiar faces such as Ronaldo and Zinedine Zidane, the Spaniards had won the competition in three of the previous five seasons. The Brazilian striker opened the scoring, but Trezeguet would equalize only to see Roberto Carlos again put the home side in front. Back in Turin, Del Piero would hand Juventus the advantage once more and Madrid would see their best chance thwarted as Luis Figo's penalty was turned away by a terrific save from Buffon.

Just moments later, it would be Pavel Nedvěd unleashing a powerful shot to crush the life from Madrid, with the Czech midfielder adding another highlight to a season he had littered with ferocious shooting. Scoring vital goals with both feet, he also offered superb play-making ability, while allying an incredible amount of effort and tenaciousness. It was a trademark goal that highlighted Nedvěd's emergence as a complete footballer and one of the best players of his generation.

Deployed on the left of midfield by Lippi, he had been granted the freedom to drift inside when Juve were in possession. So often skillful wide-men are guilty of not tracking back, but Nedvěd's workmanlike attitude made him an excellent team player, suited to a variety of tactics and positions. Able to turn a game on its head with a moment of brilliance at one end of the pitch, in his prime he would rarely be caught out as the defensive culprit at the other end. He dominated the team in 2002-03, driving them on from that wide left position and being a major influence in Europe, but victory in the semi-final against Madrid would come at a high price. A challenge on Steve McManaman on the halfway line in the dying moments would see him booked for the tackle, and find him suspended for the final against Milan.

It would be a bitter end to the season for both Nedvěd and Juventus, who never overcame the loss of their talisman at Old Trafford. Manuel Rui Costa had a goal disallowed for offside while Buffon made one of the greatest saves of his career from a point-blank range Filippo Inzaghi header. Antonio Conte came on as a substitute and headed a Del Piero cross onto the bar and then Paolo Maldini narrowly missed after finding himself unmarked at another set piece. Roque Júnior sustained an injury early in extra time, but without Nedvěd Juventus could find no way through the Milan defence.

Many fans and pundits blamed the lack-lustre performance on the absence of Nedvěd, and his contribution to the campaign was rewarded with the 2003 Balon d'Or as well as the Serie A Footballer and Foreign Footballer of the Year awards. It was fitting recognition for a truly remarkable season, but one a man like Nedvěd would exchange in heartbeat for greater team glory.

This is perhaps where the first signs of the decline of Moggi's prowess began, as unlike after previous trips to the Champions League Final, the transfer mogul would make only minimal changes to the squad. Juventus struggled to reach the same high standard as in the two previous seasons, crashing out of the Champions League to Deportivo La Coruña and suffering a raft of uncharacteristic league defeats. Lippi would depart, replacing Trapattoni as the coach of the Italian national team, and his replacement would be one of a number of surprise arrivals at Juventus in the summer of 2004.

Having sworn he would never return to the club he represented as a player, Fabio Capello incensed Roma fans by doing just that. A fine midfielder, the coach began his career with SPAL, winning promotion to the top flight with the modest club and displaying great qualities in front of the defence. Excellent at reading the game, he was strong both in the air and an effective tackler who could also make intelligent use of the ball despite an inherent lack of speed. A knee injury limited his appearances, but in 1967 he moved to Roma and became a key player for the Giallorossi, scoring six goals as he helped the club to his first ever trophy, the 1969 Coppa Italia.

After a loss to Swindon Town in the Anglo-Italian Cup, Capello was sold to Juventus, but would endure a poor start to life in Turin. After publicly criticising Armando Picchi on the same day the coach announced he was suffering from cancer, he would improve dramatically. Helping the Bianconeri to league titles in 1971–72, 1972–73, and 1974–75, he was unable to prevent Ajax from emerging victorious in the 1973 European Cup Final. His knee injuries persisted however and Juventus sent him to Milan in exchange for Romeo Benetti. Despite the transfer, in 1974 he would enjoy what he described as "the best moment" of his career.

Lining up for Italy against England at Wembley in what was the farewell match for the great Bobby Moore, few could imagine the role he would play. The World Cup-winning captain was saying goodbye after 108 internationals, but the 27 year old Capello was busy making a name for himself. As a coach he would do the same, taking over from Arrigo Sacchi at Milan and masterminding some incredible victories, before winning titles with both Real Madrid and Roma.

It was whilst with the capital club he would publicly criticize Moggi and Juventus as the two clubs battled for the league title. Capello would use a press conference to call out the Director General, inferring he was making illicit payments to agents and players. Moggi responded by claiming referees favoured Roma, citing instances where their opposition have been declined legitimate penalty claims. The Italian FA would charge the pair with 'raising suspicions about the validity of the championship'. Given their previous stances, Capello arriving to work with Moggi at Juventus seemed unthinkable, yet there he was.

The Director had seemingly pulled another masterstroke and followed it up by signing Zlatan Ibrahimović from Ajax and convincing Inter to send Fabio Cannavaro to Turin in exchange for reserve goalkeeper Fabian Carini. It was exactly the type of deal that raised questions about the Director General, now operating without restraint following the sad death of Umberto Agnelli earlier that year. Moggi began to make more and odder transfer decisions, paying Roma an extortionate amount for Emerson despite the Brazilian midfielder having only a year left on his contract.

The team marched to the Scudetto, simply too strong and too deep for their opponents, winning the title with three games remaining.

Gianni Agnelli, who was rarely photographed with Moggi, once famously justified the club's association with the director by saying "the king's stable boy must know all the horse thieves!" Now freed of the watchful eye of those two great men, this particular 'horse thief' would fill the power vacuum, leaning heavily on a player agency – GEA World – run by his son, Alessandro, to wield huge influence on the transfer market.

> *"Moggi should be considered as a sort of Godfather of Italian football, the ruler of the transfer market. It is commonly felt there wouldn't be a transfer in Italy without Moggi's consent."*
> *– Giancarlo Galavotti, Gazzetta dello Sport*

A game against Milan at San Siro in May of 2005 all but decided the destination of the title, as Trezeguet scored a winner on a wonderful assist from Del Piero. The captain was only playing due to a retrospective ban ruling out Ibrahimović, as he became an increasingly peripheral figure under the leadership of Capello. The dull, functional football may have enjoyed success at home, but in Europe it was light-years behind and Liverpool outplayed the Bianconeri over two legs of the quarter-final of the Champions League. Man for man, Juventus had a much better squad, but Rafael Benítez thoroughly out-coached and out-thought Capello in a manner many thought was impossible.

The subsequent season would follow remarkably similar lines. Moggi would take advantage of another club's financial position, paying very little to bring Giorgio Chiellini to the club from Fiorentina, but then overpaid for an over-the-hill Patrick Vieira. The French midfielder was a long time target of Moggi, yet it must have proven sweet indeed for Arsène Wenger to see his former captain look lost against Cesc Fàbregas who had taken his place. Again, it was a loss that Capello should have shouldered the blame for, but thanks to the explosive events that would follow he would soon leave the club anyway.

He would certainly not be alone.

CALCIOPOLI & A CLUB REBORN

Calciopoli. The mere mention of the word is often enough to spark a reaction from almost every Juventus supporter who lived through that tumultuous summer. The 'opoli' suffix is the Italian equivalent of the 'gate' English speakers are so fond of, adding to countless scandals from political bribery to insider trading on the stock market. This particular case, however, often referred to as Moggiopoli – a moniker even more despised by those of a Bianconeri persuasion – continues to irritate even today as new evidence is uncovered on a regular basis.

It has been eight years since the shocking story first broke, a stunning tale of alleged corruption and bribery which tore the Italian game apart, yet galvanised the national team and at least partly inspired their against-the-odds World Cup win in 2006. In that time, the critics of Serie A have used it as definitive proof in their argument that football on the peninsula is dying a slow and painful death, while its defenders fought endlessly to make clear it was never about the actual fixing of matches, more an ingrained system of influence-peddling among the power-brokers of the game.

Just as Italy prepared to face France in the deciding game of the World Cup, news began to break that the league was at the centre of a deadly power struggle. It engulfed almost every top-flight club, the Italian referees association and a number of other key figures within the game. Juventus would eventually be relegated due to the actions of Luciano Moggi, a man whose image as a corrupt and control-obsessed figure was once embraced by the club's supporters. The punishment was demotion to the second tier with a seventeen-point penalty, reduced to nine on appeal later in the year.

Having originally been recommended for relegation to Serie C2 with a thirty-point deduction, the actual punishment was either extremely harsh or far too lenient depending on little more than whether the opinion was offered by a Juventus supporter or not. A more than valid counterpoint would be that the other clubs implicated were treated much too kindly, with Milan even allowed to retain their berth in the following season's Champions League, a competition they would go on to win in May 2007.

The board of the club, including the famous 'Triade' of Antonio Giraudo, Roberto Bettega and Moggi resigned immediately, the latter doing so in tears as he told reporters not to ask him questions because "I no longer have the soul for it, they have killed it". With the focus of the trials shaped to target Juventus, the company who owned the club acted quickly and effectively plea-bargained the lesser punishment. Led by CEO John Elkann, Gianni Agnelli's grandson, the club laid the blame with those men and was viewed as weak for doing so. Yet given the clear desire to damage Juventus, it is sickening to imagine what Guido Rossi – the man leading the trials as temporary head of the Italian FA – could have done had they not taken such an approach.

"I don't have either the strength or the willingness to answer any questions. I miss my soul, it has been killed. Tomorrow I'll be resigning, since tonight the football world isn't my world anymore. I'll think only to defend myself from all allegations and wicked actions" – Luciano Moggi

Moggi continued his own 'everyone is guilty or everyone is innocent' defence, consistently his mantra throughout the intervening years. He argued he was "not the only devil in a sea of angels", maintaining other clubs had done the same things he was accused of and that he acted so as to 'protect' Juve with match officials after others had, in his mind at least, unduly influenced them. However the former Director General was eventually found guilty of sporting fraud by the Naples Judge and condemned to a five years and four month prison sentence, which due to the Italian laws regarding age and length of sentence, he will almost certainly never serve a day of. In addition, Fiorentina's owners, Diego and Andrea Della Valle, as well as Lazio President Claudio Lotito, were all found guilty and given similarly unlikely-to-be-enforced one year and three month sentences.

Former refereeing designator, Paolo Bergamo, was given three years and eight months for his involvement, while his colleague at the time, Pierluigi Pairetto – and former International official Massimo De Santis – were also found guilty and handed one year and eleven month sentences. Innocenzo Mazzini, the former Vice President of the Italian FA was condemned to two years and two months as seven other officials, including linesmen and the former Reggina President, were handed lesser sentences. Meanwhile Lecce, Bologna, Brescia, Atalanta and the consumers' society had their appeals for damages and lost revenue upheld, unlike Juventus whose similar request was rejected much to the chagrin of everyone connected with the club.

A second trial, held in July 2011, seemed set to peter out into nothing until the Italian FA's Chief Prosecutor, Stefano Palazzi, issued a statement which outlined his belief that FC Internazionale was guilty of "conduct aimed at ensuring an advantage in the standings". This sent shockwaves through the Calcio community as the original verdicts, widely criticised for their rushed and highly selective nature, perceived Moggi to be the chief instigator in a network of relationships between club management and referees throughout Italian football.

As well as forcing the Turin club into Serie B, that first case also saw the 2005-06 league title handed to the Milanese club, and here is where layers of legal terms complicate the matter considerably. The following two rules of the FIGC Code of Sporting Justice are routinely cited in the Calciopoli case:

Article One: Unsportsmanlike conduct, starting with lowly offences such as swearing or blasphemy on the pitch to excessive numbers of phone-calls to league/FA officials. Violations of this rule have previously been punished with fines or, in extreme cases, a minor points penalty.

Article Six: The attempt to gain an advantage in the standings through match-fixing or attempted match-fixing. Violations usually punishable with immediate relegation.

However, Article 18 of the code – pertaining to the punishments for breaking these rules – opens up an entire range of punishments for every article, from simply a reprimand, to going as far as removing previously won titles and relegation. In 2006, Juventus, due to a combination of hasty decisions, some dubiously positioned officials and the evidence being shaped to paint them as the ultimate villains of the piece, was handed an unprecedented relegation for numerous Article One violations.

The judgment ruled that although there was no violation of Article Six, the exclusive relationship between Moggi and certain officials constituted a clear advantage. What has happened in the intervening years, thanks largely to relentless appealing, harassing and goading of the FIGC by Moggi, is the uncovering of a wealth of new evidence. This began almost before the freshly adjusted 2006-07 season when a raft of previously unheard and unreleased Telecom Italia recordings were revealed, sparking a new trial of the whole process in Naples, often referred to as 'Calciopoli II'.

Again, thanks to Moggi and the lawyers he has personally employed, the FIGC were left with no option but to take an interest and open up the possibility of further punishments. They gave Palazzi the task of examining the new evidence, much of which revealed that former Inter President, Giacinto Facchetti, had regular contact with referees and other top football officials between 2004 and 2006. Transcripts taken from recordings revealed a continued and extensive dialogue between Facchetti and former refereeing designators Paolo Bergamo and Pierluigi Pairetto, the very men the ex-Juve Director General was constantly talking to. This, while in no way proving Moggi was innocent, clearly negated the original ruling that he enjoyed an 'exclusive relationship' with the two officials.

Palazzi had, by going on record saying Facchetti has breached Article 6, all but said that Inter's role in the corrupt system was perhaps the largest of all. Italy's Statute of Limitations states that the maximum time after an event that legal proceedings can be initiated is five years, and this has been seized upon by Moggi and conspiracy theorists as 'proof' that Inter will never be punished for their actions. Facchetti passed away before any of this new evidence was brought to light and, whilst it was tragic to see a truly iconic figure become tainted in this manner, it is only right and fair that all guilty parties are brought to justice equally. Sadly it appears this will now never happen.

The scandal and its devastating after-effects would continue to exert a hold over the club for many years, perhaps only as Antonio Conte restored the tricolore to the front of the shirt in the summer of 2012 did the healing process truly begin. It affected every aspect of the club, from sponsors who either fled or sought to renegotiate at substantially reduced rates, to the changes in the standard of personnel representing the club on the field.

After years of seeing some of world football's genuine stars grace the Torinese turf, Juventus were reduced to fielding players such as Giuliano Giannichedda and Jean-Alain Boumsong in positions once graced by some of the most famous names in the history of the game. The only exceptions were when unthinkable sums of money were guaranteed to fading stars like Fabio Cannavaro – a once classy defender, who became an embarrassment in his second stint with the club – or Amauri, a striker whose contract became a constant source of amusement and ridicule even among Juventus fans.

Jean-Claude Blanc, the CEO charged with running the club, effectively performed financial miracles, as he restored some sense of normality to the business structure. On a sporting level, the club would spiral ever deeper out of control until the arrivals of Andrea Agnelli and Director General Beppe Marotta in the summer of 2010. Before the appointment of the latter, transfer strategy was the remit of Alessio Secco, a man promoted far above his level of competency following the resignation of the entire board as the scandal broke.

Yet, for every one of those wasted years and every transfer that made a mockery of the famous 'Stilo Juve', there was one shining light that somehow made it all worthwhile. Here was a gift, which made all the talk of subterfuge and conspiracy fade into the background and become ultimately meaningless – the experience of spending the 2006-07 season in Serie B. It marked the only season the club has ever spent outside the top division, but signifies something far more intangible for anyone connected with the Turin giants.

There has never been a greater cleansing of a club in Italy than Juventus that year, and no way to explain the bonds forged between the genuine supporters who went to the stadium each week and the high quality players who remained to play second-tier football. The opposition may have been Arezzo and Modena rather than Arsenal or Madrid, but the memories of that league campaign, that quest for redemption, will remain unsurpassed for those who lived through it.

While Zlatan Ibrahimović and Patrick Vieira ensured they would forever be persona non grata in Piedmont, five of their former teammates – four of whom had just played in the World Cup Final – would secure an eternal place in the hearts of Juventini across the globe. Dubbed 'The Samurai', Alessandro Del Piero, Gigi Buffon, Pavel Nedved, David Trezeguet and Mauro Camoranesi opted to accept a responsibility they could quite easily have declined and ensure the club's restoration to European football's top table as quickly as possible.

"A true gentleman never leaves his lady"
– Alessandro Del Piero, June 2006

It would prove to be a unique experience, one perhaps unparalleled anywhere else in the world and to see these iconic names on team-sheets at stadiums where attendances usually numbered in the hundreds was truly a sight to behold. Fans occupied every available vantage point, including in one instance a hospital corridor affording a view directly into one tiny stadium, to see a team that morphed into something akin to basketball's Harlem Globetrotters.

This travelling circus of footballing brilliance won promotion at a canter, comfortably restoring pride where just a few months earlier there was only pain. They would lose just four times, only two of which came before a place in Serie A was secured and they set records for most points won (94), most consecutive wins (8) and longest winning streak in away matches (5).

Aided by his fellow stars, Del Piero would lead the league in scoring, and also netted a career milestone along the way, a strike he later described by saying: "goal number 200 with Juventus. I scored it against Frosinone and was proud to have scored against Frosinone in Serie B". He did it all with his usual humility, deflecting attention from himself to the team and its mission at every opportunity.

That was a theme which ran throughout the season and perhaps it is those untold stories which are the true legacy of that landmark year. In the vast pantheon of former Juventus greats, a name like Matteo Paro would often be overlooked by anyone with even a strong knowledge of the history of Italian football's Old Lady. But to true aficionados of history – and indeed Italian football in general – his name will be linked as intrinsically to the club as those of the World Cup and Balon d'Or winners that graced the side during its darkest hour.

At first glance, his career seems quite unremarkable, a journeyman path typically trodden by so many players who graduate from the youth systems of Serie A's top clubs. He made his first-team debut at the end of the 2003-04 season, coming on as a late substitute in a meaningless game with the title already secured. From there he was sold in co-ownership to Chievo as part of the deal to bring Nicola Legrottaglie to Juve.

Paro moved on to Crotone after just four months and would become a regular for them under Giampiero Gasperini, the man in charge of the midfielder's youth team while the pair was at Juventus. The coach continued to snap up his former players both at Crotone and later at Genoa to great effect, a trend started by the success of Paro, and his intelligent play earned him a move to top flight club AC Siena.

Buying Chievo's half-share of the then 22-year-old and entrusting him with a starting role, Siena would see their faith repaid in full as they easily avoided relegation, a feat that cannot be underestimated for one of the peninsula's perennial yo-yo clubs. Juventus of course were marching to consecutive titles under Fabio Capello, playing with the ruthless efficiency so often synonymous with the former England coach.

Then came the Calciopoli bombshell and its previously documented consequences which for Paro meant Juve buying back the entirety of his contract and Didier Deschamps placing his faith in the midfielder. His invention and defensive ability would see La Vecchia Signora breeze to the top of the table and, thanks to the efforts of the Asti native, replacing the lost duo of Emerson and Patrick Vieira was nothing like the difficult task it could and perhaps should have been.

However, it is the opening match of that campaign for which Paro will be most fondly remembered. A strange and surreal day that saw players like Gigi Buffon and David Trezeguet swap Berlin's World Cup Final for that historic first weekend in Serie B and Rimini's tiny Stadio Romeo Neri. With an hour on the clock a Pavel Nedvěd shot was blocked and, as the ball bounced loose outside the area, in came Paro, crashing a shot past the helpless goalkeeper and securing forever his place in Bianconeri lore.

The sheer joy and relief on the faces of his teammates was plain to see and the recovery had begun in earnest. His other major contribution to the club would not see the man himself looking quite so pleased however, as an injury ruled him out for a short spell in the spring. One man's misery is another's fortune as the old adage would have it, and that was definitely the case here, as the player to take his place would be Turin-born Claudio Marchisio.

Three years younger than the man he would supplant, Marchisio has gone on to become a regular for club and country and the confidence he took from playing in those Cadetti matches has been invaluable along the way. Paro, like many more prestigiously-named midfielders over the coming seasons, would never take back his place from the inspired Marchisio, but his is a place every inch as valuable in the club's story, thanks to that season of redemption.

The club would walk over the second tier competition as you would fully expect, but it was not without casualties. As the season drew to a close, talk turned to what improvements would need to be made to the squad and coach Didier Deschamps could not agree with management as to the transfer strategy. Those disagreements remained unresolved and the World Cup winner would walk away once more from Juventus, a loss bemoaned by many as the Frenchman developed into a quality manager.

SEMPRE NEL CUORE:
ALE, RICKY & GIANLUCA PESSOTTO

In the summer of 2006, Juve sealed their 29th Serie A title and Italy went on to play a memorable FIFA World Cup with several Bianconeri playing key roles in the tournament. The Scudetto and Cup took second billing to the events and fallout unfolding after Calciopoli. Whatever our opinions may be on the relegation, lifetime bans and points deduction, Juve's losses that year were far greater than any sense of sporting injustice.

While the lasting effect on the club and its star players has been thoroughly documented, it must also be remembered that numerous less heralded names felt the impact of the scandal and none more so than Gianluca Pessotto. He wasn't a glamorous headline-grabbing defender and many of his 243 appearances for La Madama went unnoticed, but the versatile left-footer was part of many of Marcello Lippi's greatest triumphs.

Blessed with neither the pace nor incisiveness of his peers, Pessotto was never a true rival for the likes of Cafu or even team-mate Gianluca Zambrotta, but he was a fine footballer who possessed an immaculate touch and an extremely high tactical intelligence, with or without the ball at his feet. Able to play as a full-back or midfielder, he managed twenty-two caps for Italy, part of the squads which took part in both the 1998 World Cup and Euro 2000. At the latter he would score in the penalty shoot-out which catapulted the Azzurri past the Netherlands and into the final where they would eventually lose out to winners France.

Spot kicks would be central to his greatest moments for the Bianconeri too, also netting from twelve yards in the 1996 Champions League Final to help his side to a memorable victory. He would end his playing career in the summer of 2006 with a medal haul to rival some of the game's greatest ever players. Adding six league titles, an Italian Cup and no less than seven other major honours to that European Cup win over Ajax, Pessotto should have been able to look back on a wonderful career with pride and satisfaction.

Instead, Calciopoli would perhaps claim him as the most affected victim, leaving him unable to balance his efforts on the field with the accusations laid out in court against Juventus. As the entire board resigned in the wake of the initial allegations, Pessotto took up a role as a director, seeking to once again provide a reliable hand to help steer the club through a difficult period. The whole affair would be too much for him to handle however and, on the morning of June 27 that year, he was discovered in the street outside Juve's headquarters clutching rosary beads, having apparently thrown himself from a dormer window in the roof fifteen metres above.

"Everything I had done on the pitch had just disappeared; it was like receiving a kick to the head without knowing where it had come from. I felt like the victim of persecution as I was being chased as if I was the worst offender. Every person I saw seemed like the Devil or the Madonna.

"I was up at the club's headquarters and I wanted to go home. I switched off the light and I woke up eight or nine days later. When I woke up, a psychiatrist explained everything to me. I couldn't eat for three or four days as I tried to understand what had happened." – Pessotto to La Stampa in 2008

The incident would cast a long shadow over the Italian camp preparing for the World Cup quarter-final, with a Fabio Cannavaro press conference the moment the players learnt news of what had happened. One of five Juventus players in the squad, the Azzurri captain was laughing and joking with reporters when he heard. "I'm devastated. Pessotto was the nicest guy in the world", he said before leaving abruptly as Alessandro Del Piero, Zambrotta and Ciro Ferrara flew back to visit their former team-mate in hospital. A few days later Pessotto's wife Reana confirmed the worst, telling ANSA;

"He was very much suffering because of the football scandal and the fact that Juve was a part of it. He said that it was unfair, and that his work counted for nothing now. The fatigue, the sadness for his club's situation, all of that added up. He became very fragile, he was very depressed because of the role he had inside the club. It wasn't as fun as he thought it would be. More than a month ago, he started going to the office with no pleasure at all. He realised that this is not what he was supposed to do with his life".

Suffering multiple fractures and internal bleeding, it was an enormous relief when his doctors announced he was making good progress, particularly for his friends in Germany who had paraded a banner declaring "Pessottino, we are with you!" after securing passage to the semi-finals. Later he would describe his own mental state as "a delicate road", but as soon as he was able the club welcomed him back into the Juventus family, helping him to slowly recover and rebuild his life.

Re-integrated in a role as team manager, he was eventually promoted to a position in charge of youth development department and said he was thankful he had been able to bridge the gap that became so unbearable that fateful summer day. "I hope to transmit experience and above all passion", he said of his new role. "But it will be a reciprocal thing. They will give me enthusiasm, dreams and emotions."

While his own dreams were shattered by Calciopoli, even his fragile state of mind would fade into the background following what would transpire at the club's training ground on December 15, 2006, adding to the feeling that this was indeed the blackest of years. Heading back inside after a hard day's Primavera training, concerned team-mates raised the alarm after noticing the clothing and bags of Alessio Ferramosca (aged just 17) and Riccardo Neri (16) untouched in the locker room and being unable to find the two youngsters.

They were eventually discovered by divers from the Turin fire brigade, who pulled the two boys from an artificial lake near the club house at Vinovo. Sadly, it seemed Alessio and Riccardo chased a lost football onto the plastic sheeting that covered the water. The lake measured 50 x 30 feet and was built to collect rain water to lessen the facility's impact on the environment.

When they were recovered, it was too late. Ferramosca, in addition to hypothermia, had suffered cardiac arrest and was immediately pronounced dead. Neri, whose body temperature had dropped to 20oC, was taken to hospital where attempts to revive him continued until midnight, tragically to no avail. The club immediately cancelled its Serie B tie with Cesena – scheduled for the same day – while all levels of the Youth Sector would contest no fixtures for almost two weeks.

Investigators ascertained that the two youngsters had stood at the edge of the lake attempting to recover lost footballs from training, only to slip on the covering sheet. They were unable to determine whether they fell in together, or if one fell first and the other followed while attempting to save his friend.

So talented were the pair, and their generation, that their Berretti side – a now disbanded Under-17 team – was already five points clear of the standings. Ferramosca was a talented midfield prospect who arrived at Juventus that same summer, moving from local amateur club Atletico Mirafiori where his father was President. He had celebrated his seventeenth birthday at the club just three months before and had been enrolled in a local school.

Neri, born in Florence, was an even greater prospect and arrived at in Turin two years earlier from Empoli. In June he helped the Giovanissimi Nazionali (Under-15s) team win their own Scudetto, saving the decisive penalty against Perugia. He had made a huge impression on Michelangelo Rampulla, former Juve player and the first-team goalkeeping coach at the time. Speaking to him about Neri, Rampulla told me in 2010:

"He had great qualities. That year he won the championship and grew very well physically and technically. We had already thought of taking him with us into the first team after Viareggio and train him personally."

It is well worth remembering that the only other keeper behind Gianluigi Buffon at that time was Antonio Chimenti and it is more than plausible Neri would have become a familiar face to us all had he not lost his life in such terrible circumstances. Their joint funeral was held at Turin Cathedral and was attended by well over a thousand people, including many young people from both the Juventus youth teams and their schools, some first team players, the club management and representatives of other teams.

There was still a huge feeling of shock and sadness, emotions that only intensified when the white coffin of Neri was carried in, draped with his number one shirt and two scarves: the black and white of Juventus and another in the Viola of his beloved Fiorentina. Gianluca Zambrotta, by then at Barcelona but still in attendance, was visibly moved when Ferramosca's coffin followed his companion's up to the altar.

The club made clear its intention to honour their memory and continues to do so even today. The pitch where the Primavera plays their home games has been named 'Campo Ale e Ricky' after them and a huge mosaic of the pair – commissioned by local artist Leonardo Pivi – is next to the field.

Supporters regularly make efforts to do the same, and on one occasion passed out 22,000 golden flags at a match against Milan at the Stadio Olimpico, while the 'Alessio Ferramosca e Riccardo Neri foundation' also holds many events to preserve their memory. Charity dinners were also held and by 2007 the club announced plans to host an annual tournament for under-15 sides to be held at Vinovo.

It was aptly named the 'Ale & Ricky Sempre nel Cuore' tournament.

Ciro Immobile, a former teammate of the two youngsters, finds Ale and Ricky impossible to forget. Shortly after making his UEFA Champions League debut at Bordeaux with the Juventus first-team, the forward dedicated his performance at the 2010 Viareggio Tournament to the pair. Scoring an all-time record ten goals at the event and being named player of the tournament, Immobile netted in the final and told RAI Sport during the celebrations:

"This victory is dedicated to Alessio Ferramosca and Riccardo Neri. They are in our hearts and they are always with us, from up above they helped us win. This Viareggio has been unforgettable: for the team, for me and because of them."

From that tragic moment right up until the present day, Ale and Ricky's memory has remained with everyone and their legacy will never fade. All it took was a bad pass, a ball rolling in the wrong place. Darkness, slippery ground and freezing water. A ball which seemed destined to give them a bright and happy future instead united them in tragedy. Alessio and Riccardo left us one last time to chase their great love of that ball which fuels the hopes and dreams of so many of us as children. They must never be forgotten.

ALESSANDRO DEL PIERO: THE GREATEST OF ALL TIMES

"Three players can be considered Juventus symbols: Boniperti, Platini and certainly Del Piero. I'll always be grateful to Alessandro, like all our fans are." – Andrea Agnelli, May 2012

It began on a nondescript autumn day, a typically drab and grey Turin afternoon, at the much-despised Stadio delle Alpi. Slender, with an uncontrolled mop of hair, he entered the field as an unnecessary substitute in what was an ultimately meaningless game. The crowd greeted him with almost an air of indifference, seemingly challenging him to prove he was worthy of the praise his yet-to-be realised potential had already garnered.

It would end close to nineteen years later, in almost exactly the same place; yet, if Alessandro Del Piero's final appearance in the proud colours of his beloved Juventus proved one thing, it was the old adage that the more things change, the more they truly do remain the same. It was no longer the cold chill of winter that approached, but the spring sunshine acting as a makeshift spotlight on the final moments of the great captain's career while simultaneously dispersing the shadows that had once engulfed the grand Old Lady of Italian football. From the dominance of Silvio Berlusconi's all-conquering Milan of the late 1980s and early '90s to the despair of Calciopoli and its devastating aftermath, Del Piero had guided Juventus past it all, beating off some serious personal adversity along the way.

Juventus have had truly great captains before, men who led the club with a powerful blend of grace, dignity and a will to win that ordinary players could only dream of aspiring to. Men such as Giampiero Boniperti, Michel Platini and Gaetano Scirea – whose names even today are revered among younger supporters who never saw them – all came before him, but Del Piero would first embrace each of those traditions before eventually becoming part of them himself.

The son of an electrician, he was born in the small Veneto town of Conegliano and quickly caught the eye of scouts across the peninsula. Yet he almost never arrived at the club with which he would become synonymous. "Before joining Padova at 13, I had a trial some months earlier to go and play in Turin... but at its other club, Torino!", Del

Piero once told *France Football*. "At the time they had probably the best academy in Italy. But my mother was categorical: 'You're only 12. You're too young and Turin is a long way away'."

A brief spell with Padova in Serie B followed, during which – according to an urban legend – a Juventus scout famously came to watch one of his games. Feeling unimpressed, he left a quarter of an hour from the end with Del Piero promptly scoring twice after his exit. Fittingly, it would be Giampiero Boniperti – then the President of Juventus – who bought the player who would go on to break his scoring records for the lowly sum of just five billion lire, today's equivalent of £2.2 million. Writing in his own book, the older man said, "I immediately took him to see the trophies. 'Have you seen how many we have won?', I asked. 'I hope that you can contribute to making Juventus even greater'."

Del Piero began that quest like a hurricane, scoring goals almost immediately. His debut came against Foggia and just a week later netted his first goal in the famous black and white stripes. That goal, against Reggiana, convinced Giovanni Trapattoni to give him his first start and the coach's faith was duly rewarded with a hat-trick. He was only just beginning to show what he could and would do.

Sometimes a moment changes forever the perception of a person and the first of those in the career of Alessandro Del Piero would come on December 4, 1994. Juve trailed Fiorentina 2-0 when his pass released Ravanelli down the left and Vialli headed home. Ever the professional, the former Sampdoria star grabbed the ball from the back of the net and never even celebrated his goal, running back up field. Game on. Following a corner and a drastic scramble to clear the ball by Fiorentina, the ball came back into the box. Del Piero and Ravanelli were both unable to control it, but there was Vialli again to thump home the equaliser. This time he enjoyed it, two goals that had seen him drag his side back from the brink of defeat to a hard earned point.

And then it happened.

With time running out and the game petering out into a draw, Alessandro Orlando punted another ball into the Viola box, more in hope than expectation, but this was now the perfect stage for the *talented youngster* to showcase his ability to the world. Where most people may try to control a ball travelling that distance and dropping over his shoulder, Del Piero executed a volley that was, in one instant, both utterly simple and breathtakingly brilliant.

The two defenders in close attendance stood no chance, goalkeeper Francesco Toldo even less. Claudio Ranieri on the Fiorentina bench had that same look of resigned dignity he has since perfected and a great career was launched. From there he became the player of choice for Marcello Lippi who instigated the sale of Roberto Baggio to Milan and handed the number ten shirt to his young apprentice. Some goals do more than win three points and for Alessandro Del Piero this one gave birth to a legend.

His first five seasons would see him emerge as just that, scoring goal after goal as the team won three league titles, an Italian Cup, the Champions League, a UEFA Cup and the 1996 World Club Championship, a game which did for him what the 1985 version did for the club he cherished. Still just 22 years old, the striker had continued to shine, a string of fantastic strikes following that remarkable volley against the Viola. But, just as Juventus became kings of Europe, Vialli and Ravenelli were allowed to leave as Zinedine Zidane arrived.

Lippi had by now firmly placed his trust in his new-found star and the team headed to Tokyo for an edition of the Intercontinental Cup that would, unlike some years, be a true event. Italy's grandest club would face Argentinian giants River Plate, a side which contained some famous names of its own that would go on to grace European football over the next decade. Juan Pablo Sorín, Marcelo Salas, Julio Cruz and Ariel Ortega lined up with the classy Enzo Francescoli but, while Del Piero had started on his path to stardom, this game would crown his arrival as a true star of world football.

Juve had controlled the game, creating a seemingly endless number of chances for Alen Bokšić, but it remained delicately balanced until, with nine minutes left on the clock, a corner from Angelo Di Livio was headed across the six-yard box by Zidane. It fell to a completely and inexplicably unmarked Del Piero who swivelled to fire an unstoppable shot high into the roof of the net. It ended River Plate's hopes but ignited the scorer, his meteoric rise now seemingly having no limits.

The young man was thriving, renowned for a strike from the edge of the area that came to be called the 'zona Del Piero', but then his world collapsed. Travelling to Udine on November 8, 1998, the Bianconeri played out a 2-2 draw, but the game was far from being the story. Turning to bear down on goal in, Del Piero inexplicably collapsed onto the Stadio Friuli turf, clutching his knee. After bursting into tears at the realisation he was seriously injured, Del Piero was stretchered from the field. Nobody present that day would realise until later just how serious that injury was.

The hopes of the club departed with their number ten and Juventus limped to a lowly sixth place finish. It would take nine months of hard work for the captain to be fit again and he would not feature for Juventus again until August 4, 1999. Of course he scored on his return but it took perhaps another year – some would argue it was much much longer – before he was anywhere near the player he was before that injury.

He struggled to contribute, no longer the explosive talent who challenged Ronaldo to be the planet's premier player. He would fail to net from open play until a game against Parma towards the end of that campaign. Del Piero was a ghost during Italy's Euro 2000 journey, eventually becoming the scapegoat for the Azzurri's ultimate failure. Gianni Agnelli began referring to him as 'Godot', the title character who never arrives in the Samuel Beckett play, a harsh assessment for a player who came to embody the club itself, many unable to remember a time without him. Yet part of what made him so great was that he himself remembered and constantly referred to those who came before in the same awestruck tone with which he is now revered.

"Del Piero is a champion with extraordinary technical ability and wonderful characteristics. When he is selected he never disappoints. He is an example to us all with great skills and intuitions that few other players have. He is a captain in the real sense of the word"– Marcello Lippi, May 2012

His own legacy was being discussed and recounted, as many wondered if he could ever return to those former heights. The years passed but finally, in one defining moment, he would return. Of course he has scored better goals; of course he has scored more important goals. Alessandro Del Piero has netted vital strikes at the World Cup, in a Champions League Final, in the World Club Cup Final and has won so many top trophies and titles that his list of personal honours is longer than that of most clubs. The all-time leading goal scorer in the history of Italy's grandest club has, as they say, been there, done it and has enough medals to put on the table to silence even Alan Hansen.

Many people feel strong connections to footballers they idolise as children, but this author's personal feelings towards Del Piero are slightly different. While still young, I loved Gaetano Scirea and Franco Baresi. While clearly not a classy central defender, Del Piero and I are a similar age and as I grew up watching him do the same in a much more public manner, I felt a bond that no other athlete has ever given me. I felt his pain as I looked on during that fateful day in Udine when his knee first gave way; I suffered with him as he squandered a gilt-edged chance to seal victory for Italy over France in the final of Euro 2000.

But before the goals, the adulation and the armband, even before he first wore the famous *Bianconeri* shirt, he was just a boy playing football with his father. Before Gianni Agnelli christened him Pinturicchio, 'our Ale' was simply Gino's son. Their bond was no greater than that which any father has with their son but, just as Del Piero finally looked to be putting the terrible injuries of his career behind him, his world was turned upside down as the man he always turned to in times of difficulty passed away.

When my own father died in January of the same year my world collapsed. The one person who had been there for me forever was gone and I retreated from life completely, lost and unsure of where to turn. Gradually I put the pain aside and began to do normal things once more, including watching football, and it was the best decision I ever made. Having heard the terrible news of Gino Del Piero's passing, it stunned me that just four days after the funeral, Ale would be among the substitutes on February 17, 2001 for a match away to southern side Bari. After 63 minutes of an exciting but scoreless game in which both sides had been denied by some fantastic goalkeeping from Jean Francois Gillet and Edwin van der Sar, Carlo Ancelotti brought on Del Piero for Darko Kovačević.

The next fifteen minutes from Del Piero were a perfect encapsulation of the way I had felt for the previous month. While my own melancholy and grief was private and hidden, I watched on as a man, who just three years earlier was arguably the world's best footballer, lived out his own in front of a packed stadium and a huge televised audience. The once immaculate first touch was gone, his passing simply terrible and shooting even worse.

Then, with less than ten minutes remaining, everything changed. The ball broke to Del Piero midway inside Bari's half, out by the left touchline. He ran directly at his marker, forcing him to back-pedal all the way into box, where a step-over left the defender flat-footed and, one touch later, the number 10 chipped a left footed shot over the advancing keeper from an acute angle to score a wonderful goal.

As he curled away, the emotion came pouring out. First, he threw Alessandro Birindelli to the ground and kicked over an advertising prop, all the while screaming in a mixture of joy, relief and sadness, before finally collapsing into the embrace of Gianluca Pessotto.

Asked in 2003 about the loss of his father, the goal and the effect it had on his life, Del Piero said;

"Undoubtedly, the death of my father had an effect on me at the time and continues to do so. But it also gave me back completely to football. I believe I've grown up, living through experiences that have opened my eyes."

Two straight league titles followed, but Del Piero was now robbed of his acceleration and top speed, so he compensated with immense technique and intelligence. He turned 30 and, as Fabio Capello arrived he found himself benched in favour of Zlatan Ibrahimović and David Trezeguet. It seemed his time in Turin was over, as he became Serie A's most substituted player and once more his place became subject of national debate. Then Calciopoli broke and Del Piero was able to cement his status as a living legend by displaying an unprecedented loyalty as he led Juve back to Serie A.

Over time, he surpassed Scirea as Juve's all-time leader in appearances, but what Alessandro Del Piero means to Juventus and her fans is not quantifiable in mere words or numbers. It is not reflected in merely the record number of goals or appearances he has made for the club; nor in the eighteen major trophies he won, or number of finals he contested. Instead it is a feeling, the kind of unconditional love we reserve for our children, parents and other close family members. He is one of them – one of us – a Juventino, perhaps the one person who embodies that concept more than any other.

I feel we can say this, knowing whole-heartedly that it will be difficult to feel greater affection or appreciation for any other player, past or present. There have of course been arguably better footballers such as Diego Maradona, whose skills were truly breath-taking. There have been better goal scorers, the likes of Marco Van Basten, even the eternally frustrating Fillipo Inzaghi.

The appreciation of Del Piero transcends sport. He is admired greatly as a player, many believing him to be both more effective and more consistent than many of his peers, such as Zinedine Zidane or Francesco Totti. He is admired as a man; his dignity, loyalty and professionalism are sadly lacking in most current players. As we have seen, his contributions have changed, ranging from being the undeniably best player between 1996 and 1998 to being only a squad player by 2005 under Fabio Capello.

That situation was repeated under Antonio Conte in his final season, but there are two actions that stand out from the many in his glorious career, the first of which is his role at the 2006 World Cup. Del Piero accepted his role as a substitute with a wonderful sense of professionalism and a firmly held belief that his chance would come typified by two instantly recognisable incidents.

Francesco Totti's winning penalty, late in the second-round match against Australia is the first. Del Piero raced fully fifty yards to be the first player to celebrate with the scorer; the very player in his starting slot and beloved number ten shirt. The other was the semi-final match versus the hosts, Germany. Upon being told yet again he would not be starting, he responded in the greatest possible manner. After being thrown on for central midfielder Simone Perrotta, he covered the defensive role perfectly then, in an Azzurri counter attack, he ran the length of the pitch to hit a first time curling shot into the top corner. It made the game two-nil to Italy, sealing the tie and the Azzurri's place in the World Cup Final for the first time since 1994.

Finally is the example he set as captain during the Calciopoli scandal later that same summer. Del Piero never once complaining at all he had lost, never bemoaning former teammates for abandoning La Vecchia Signora at her most vulnerable moment. When other high-profile players demanded transfers, Ale remained silent. At just the right time, when Juventini across the globe despaired at the demise of our illustrious club, up stepped our captain. He pledged his undying loyalty to the club and its tifosi. He told stories of his first Bianconeri shirt as a child, and of the sense of belonging it gave him. Here was possibly our greatest hero, a World Cup and Champions League winner, talking as one of us, a fan.

For these selfless acts, for these two instances of loyalty, love and devotion, I can say this man, this player is, as Muhammad Ali would have it, the greatest of all times.

His career would again come into question as he entered the twilight of his career, but he continued to break records seemingly every time he stepped onto the pitch. "Boniperti always said that if I beat him he will be happy and I am sure his joy is sincere", reflected Del Piero after equalling Boniperti's tally of 178 goals in Serie A in 2010. Four years after breaking the same man's overall record he had finally surpassed him in the league and Boniperti published a praise-filled open letter in la Gazzetta dello Sport the next day.

"I am not a liar and I will tell you straight away that it annoyed me a little bit", wrote Boniperti. "But the fact that it is you, you that I have known you since you were a little boy and you that I brought to Juve gives me satisfaction. Sooner or later it had to happen also because I stopped playing football when I hadn't yet reached 33 years, while I see that you, nearly 36, still have a great desire to train."

He continued to do just that and Del Piero's time with the Bianconeri would not come to an end until 2012, when the club and the man himself decided that a move elsewhere would prove mutually beneficial. It was handled poorly by all concerned, but his final home game would prove to be the last match of the 2011-12 season. There, laden with scarves, he basked in the adulation of the Juventus fans one last time. It was to be a final lap of honour for a man who had become their hero during his long and distinguished career. He had played before them on more than 700 occasions in the previous nineteen years, but now it was to be over. While many claim that no player is bigger than his club, or the game, Alessandro Del Piero was just that on this one May afternoon.

As the 37-year-old slowly made his way around the field, taking his time to thank the 41,000 in attendance, the game that was still taking place had become little more than a sideshow. In some ways, the fans had not really come to see the match – the previous week's victory over Cagliari had already secured the long-awaited league title. They had come to bid farewell to a player who had remained loyal through good times and bad, just as they had. Del Piero had opted to remain in Turin when Juventus were relegated in 2006 and resisted Fabio Capello's attempts to move him on. The supporters stood by their idol as he struggled to rediscover his form following countless injuries, even as the rest of the country pinned their Euro 2000 final defeat on his inability to finish a number of gilt-edged chances against France.

He was one of them, a player who embodied the spirit of Juventus in their eyes. Seen as the apprentice to Roberto Baggio in his early days, he had gone from being a natural successor to Baggio and his predecessor Michel Platini to surpassing the achievements of both men. The club's all-time leading goal scorer and appearance maker, he holds no fewer than nineteen other individual records and, were it not for the uncertain status of the two titles revoked during the Calciopoli trials, would have a record eight Scudetti.

"I am moved by Del Piero as he represents something indelible. He is the history of Juventus. That is thanks to the player and the man, so I can only thank him." – Antonio Conte

However, no amount of silverware or cold statistics can highlight his significance to the club and its fan base as aptly as the farewell he received when he called time on his glorious career. In many ways, it was just another typical performance from the man dubbed 'Pinturicchio' by the great Gianni Agnelli, painting a final delicate masterpiece at the end of yet another successful campaign and capping it with a well-struck goal from just outside the area.

After what must have been one of the most drawn-out substitutions in football history, in which Del Piero bowed to each corner of the ground before shaking hands with every member of the Juventus squad, came the most powerful outpouring of support I have ever witnessed at a sporting event. Twice, the modest captain stood from his seat on the bench to acknowledge the crowd, but they let him know that they wanted more than just a wave of farewell.

And so, with a hint of embarrassment he began his lap of the pitch, forced to pretend to tie his bootlace so onlookers could not see his tears, while a standing ovation continued unabated for almost twenty minutes. "In the next 150 years there will not be anyone like Del Piero", said Gigi Buffon after the game and it is impossible to imagine the goalkeeper being proven wrong. Del Piero played on in Sydney, but at Juventus the number ten shirt, once filled by arguably the finest Juventino of all, remained empty for a season. His departure was the hardest of farewells, but we at least had the opportunity to say goodbye. For that, we can always be thankful.

He truly was the greatest.

THE FIVE SAMURAI

"Juventus have given me everything. I acquired my winning mentality here; the one which makes you say every game is a battle. I've learnt to be demanding with myself and how to meet difficulties and overcome them. As for myself, I've given them all my time and I've put myself at the service of the team. I hope I'll leave them with something positive." – Pavel Nedvěd

It was the kind of welcome usually reserved for a Papal visit or the arrival of the Queen. A special edition of the city's newspaper had been printed, all police leave had been cancelled and the streets were bedecked in red and white ribbons. Everywhere you turned, there were people of all ages wearing tee-shirts proclaiming 'I was there!' along with the date – Saturday September 9 – and the name of AC Rimini's home, the Stadio Romeo Neri.

A tiny 9,768 capacity stadium on the picturesque Adriatic Coast, it has rarely been anywhere near full on match days since its inauguration in 1934. Thousands of balloons could not mask its dilapidated state as fans desperate for a vantage point scaled its walls, having given up on finding a ticket. Hundreds of others had camped outside since Thursday night in order to secure themselves a seat, and the official attendance would eventually be quoted as an extremely conservative estimate of 10,500. Clearly, nobody wanted to miss this match.

Rimini had never reached the top division in Italy, and this was the first time in twenty five years they had reached Serie B, yet despite the partisan atmosphere, the crowds were not there for them. Shortly before the scheduled kick-off time, the visiting team ran out onto the pitch and the crowd erupted. Their all-black kit was as unfamiliar as the names of some of those wearing it, but the welcome was one all too familiar to Juventus.

As they had been countless times before, the arrival of Juventus was feted and at first glance it appeared once again the fans of a small town club were turning out in record numbers to witness one of football's true giants. Since the Calciopoli scandal had broken a few months earlier, the subsequent relegation of Italian football's grandest side had sparked a sequence of events that very few teams in any sport have ever been subjected to.

The choice of kit colour was apt, for this was most definitely a club in mourning. The entire board resigned and were replaced and the punishment of enforced relegation with a seventeen-point penalty came to be regarded as purgatory. No sooner had Luciano Moggi's misdeeds been made public when many of world football's biggest names had fled. Among a lengthy list, Zlatan Ibrahimović, Adrian Mutu and Gianluca Zambrotta were all sold, some at their own request, but also by necessity as the new management strove to keep the club financially afloat.

Their absence meant that names such as Giuliano Giannichedda, Felice Piccolo and Dario Venitucci would regularly find themselves onto team-sheets during that season spent in the second division. Stripped of the title, they would suffer the indignity of seeing bitter rivals Inter stitch the Italian tricolore onto their own shirts to identify them the reigning champions. The departed players were lambasted in public for the first time that afternoon, the small number of visiting fans in Rimini unfurling banners vilifying them as 'mercenaries without honour'. Seen as traitors and cowards by Juventus fans, they put their own careers first and abandoned La Vecchia Signora without a second thought.

But what of those who stayed, the heroes who have become a part of club legend, names that will be forever loved by the Bianconeri faithful?

Their choice to make a stand and remain was recognised instantly by those on the Curva Scirea, who christened them the 'Samurai.' The club's fans lauded them as noble warriors, willing to give everything they had for the cause. Of course this was steeped in hyperbole, not least because two of the five men viewed in these terms were all but forced to stay against their will. Yet there is no denying the galvanising effect that keeping four protagonists of that same summer's World Cup Final – and a Balon d'Or winner – had upon the city and the club's global fan base.

Defiantly they would pull on a small black wristband bearing the club logo and the green, white and red stripes of the Italian flag. It was a small statement, but one which would serve to remind the players of their place and spur them on to fight when the world seemed to be uniting against them. A gesture that, would in turn, grow to be hugely significant for Alessandro Del Piero, Mauro Camoranesi, Gianluigi Buffon, Pavel Nedvěd and David Trezeguet. All five men will forever have the full gratitude and respect of Juventus supporters after stepping out together on that historic first weekend in Serie B.

Both John and Lapo Elkann took their seats in the stand to watch that day showing solidarity with the cause, the latter going so far as to join the players in wearing one of the wristbands. It is somewhat ironic to note that, despite later evidence unveiled against him, everyone present would impeccably observe a minutes silence before kick-off in honour of Inter legend Giacinto Facchetti who passed away a few days earlier.

Juventus started brightly with Nedvĕd shooting from distance in the second minute, the kind of opportunity that had been the hallmark of his glittering career. A few minutes later the Czech legend linked with Marco Marchionni to cross for Marcello Zalayeta who saw a header well saved. Another cross from Marchionni saw the Uruguayan striker make a spectacular attempt at an overhead kick that missed the ball completely. The chances continued, but somehow, inspired by the vociferous crowd, Rimini held on and the first half ended scoreless despite Juve's obvious domination.

There were no changes at half-time and Del Piero was closed down well after Zalayeta found his way to the byeline and clipped the ball back towards the penalty spot. In the 60th minute they would finally take the lead, another Nedvĕd effort rebounding to the edge of the box to the unmarked Matteo Paro, who fired home a well struck shot. Buffon then made a fine save from Jeda before Domenico Cristiano was sent off for a challenge on Nedvĕd. With the advantage, Juventus again pressed forward, the Balon d'Or winner unleashing one more pile-driver that was well saved.

And then it happened. Where once there was Lilian Thuram and Fabio Cannavaro, Jean-Alain Boumsong offered little of the same quality in central defence. He hesitated in dealing with a routine ball and that allowed Adrian Ricchiuti to run into the penalty area unchecked and slide the ball coolly past Buffon. At 1-1, Juventus searched in vain for a winner with Nedvĕd, Camoranesi, Zalayeta and Raffaele Palladino all squandering chances to seal the points.

Rimini exploded like they themselves had won the World Cup. Fans partied, the players unbelievably taking a lap of honour and the stadium announcer, incoherent for what seemed like forever, was beside himself with joy. The celebrations continued in the centre of town where car horns hooted and scooters weaved with glee. Everyone wanted to be part of their team's special moment

While the Biancorosso squad would go on to spend most of the ensuing season battling against relegation, Juventus expected so much more. Perhaps Buffon best summed up their collective state of mind in a brief post-match interview with Italian state broadcaster RAI. "We have to forget all the success we have achieved and dive into this new adventure", said the goalkeeper. "Nobody is giving you anything for free here in Serie B. We will have twenty more away games like this at Rimini, small stadiums where home fans can become an important factor. We have to be ready for it."

But ready for it they were, with long-time club captain Del Piero seemingly entering the best form of his career after that relegation. He had spent the previous two years suffering as a second-class citizen under Fabio Capello, the former Milan coach using him almost exclusively as a substitute – or indeed substituting him – in almost every game. Yet the classy number ten would lead his beloved club back to Serie A the only way he knew how. Week after week he would fire them past stubborn opponents, ending the campaign as the division's top scorer with twenty goals.

He would net 21 a year later, emulating fellow World Cup winner Paolo Rossi in becoming only the second man in history to top the scoring charts in the second division then the top flight in successive seasons. Over the following five years he broke a seemingly endless list of records, taking over as the all-time leading appearance maker and goal scorer, a remarkable feat given the huge history of the club. He has also thrived in continental competition, receiving a standing ovation at Real Madrid's Santiago Bernabéu following a consummate Champions League performance.

David Trezeguet trod a very similar path to Del Piero following his arrival in Turin, shortly after firing France to glory at Italy's expense. His golden goal in the Euro 2000 Final announced his arrival on the world stage, but Moggi had already seen enough to sign him from Monaco before the tournament even began. Perhaps he was always destined to be a Juventus hero. There are almost too many similarities between his life and career which echo those who have honoured the famous black and white stripes before him to simply be coincidence.

His career began at Monaco in 1995. In the principality "Trezegol" scored 52 goals in 93 Ligue 1 appearances and won two Ligue 1 championships playing alongside Thierry Henry. The two formed a superb strike partnership in the Principality before the Arsenal legend joined the Bianconeri for a short spell, but it was hoped Trezeguet would fare much better.

Yet his international heroics were not enough to prevent him from having to kick his heels on the bench at Juventus in his debut campaign. The presence of Filippo Inzaghi restricted his appearances but, much like the departure of Roberto Baggio freed Del Piero to grow into the hero we now remember, selling Inzaghi to Milan revealed just how great a striker Trezeguet could be. The very next season saw him net 32 goals, including a Serie A high 24, which saw him become Juve's first Capocannonieri since compatriot Michel Platini back in 1985.

The anti-Trezeguet camp can point to many factors as to why he cannot be considered a true great. Almost all of his goals come inside the box, ranking alongside Gary Lineker – and indeed Inzaghi – in terms of simple tap in finishes. His contribution to team play and defending was, at best, minimal. He was often guilty of being forgotten on the pitch; you could watch a Juventus game during his time at the club and, for 89 minutes, not notice whether he was actually on the field.

However it seems this very trait is his strength, as in the minute you did notice him was when he appeared between two defenders to score the inevitable and decisive goal. Over the ensuing seasons he would continue to deliver those goals with assured regularity, eventually surpassing Omar Sívori to become the club's all-time leading foreign goalscorer with 171 goals. The stats speak for themselves; his goals for Juve came in just 318 games, a phenomenal strike rate of 0.54 goals per game. Despite often being overlooked in favour of other players internationally, Trezeguet has still managed to be France's third highest ever goal scorer behind Henry and Michel Platini, with 34 goals in 71 games.

A combination of his high value and a terrible agent saw him linked with a seemingly endless list of moves away, but he remained in Turin until 2010 when he departed for Spanish club Hércules CF. Releasing the World Cup winning hit-man was seen in many quarters as a hasty move, but it was essentially driven by the players desire to move to his wife's home town and coincided with the clubs need to reduce the wage bill.

His departure could definitely have been handled better however, and Trezeguet certainly deserved to return for the chance to bid a proper 'adieu' to a fan base who adore him greatly to this day. He was given that in December 2013, making his first appearance at Juventus Stadium and being given the reception befitting such a hero.

Much like the former Monaco man, Mauro Camoranesi was constantly linked with moves away in the summer of 2006, courtesy of another less-than-dignified agent. Yet he too remained and made some spectacular contributions, not least of which was a consummate display against Lecce game during that season spent in Serie B.

Back-heeling the ball through the legs of a defender with a move reminiscent of Johan Cryuff, Camoranesi collected it and crossed for Raffaele Palladino to score.

He had come to Juventus from Hellas Verona, where he impressed enough not only to convince Moggi to sign him, but to press Marcello Lippi into converting Zambrotta into a fullback in order to get the pair in the team together. With the coach believing in his ability Camoranesi would not disappoint, combining technical skill and dribbling ability with the incredible work ethic that has always been instilled in the best Juventus players. His debut season with the club saw the team win the Scudetto, but lose the Champions League Final to Milan at Old Trafford.

More titles would follow as he established himself as one of the best midfielders in Serie A, yet he would be continually overlooked by his native Argentina. It would not take long for Italy to call him up, making Camoranesi the first 'Oriundo' in almost forty years to represent the Azzurri. When Lippi replaced Giovanni Trapattoni as national team coach, he would become a regular on the right wing and play a vital role in their triumph in Germany.

"I did not want to stay, but Juventus would not let me go", he told TuttoSport when asked about staying after the relegation. "I agreed a deal with Lyon, but I was obliged to remain. I was thirty years old and playing in Serie B, that's not really what I was dreaming of at this point of my career." The love of the fans and a desire to repay what the club had given him changed his mind and, after returning to the top flight, his efforts in the 2007-08 Serie A season earned him the prestigious Guerin d'Oro award.

After that, however, he suffered numerous injuries and his form waned drastically. It was no surprise that he too was sold on in the summer of 2010, moving to Bundesliga side VfB Stuttgart. Their struggles in the early part of the season resulted in a coaching change and the new man found no place for him and consequentially his contract was annulled. At the beginning of the following February he signed for Club Atlético Lanús in his native Argentina. Both before and after his time in Bianconeri, Camoranesi was very much a journeyman footballer, but found a home in Turin and won almost every honour the game has to offer. Again, much like with Trezeguet, the chance for a proper farewell should be extended to a player who undeniably gave his all to the Old Lady.

That opportunity was most certainly afforded to Pavel Nedvěd. The emotional scenes of his final game, when he captained the side against his former club Lazio, will live long in the memory. At full time the whole squad returned to the pitch wearing shirts inscribed with Nedvěd's name and synonymous number 11 in order to pay homage to the retiring legend.

"After everything the club had made possible for me, I felt I owed them", he said in a 2009 interview looking back on that season in Serie B. "Because of that, staying was a completely natural choice. Besides, what will I say to a young child in Turin streets if he asked me why I have abandoned Juve?" The 2003 Balon d'Or winner combined with Trezeguet and Del Piero to score 47 of the 83 goals Juve scored in Serie B to earn that promotion, continually displaying the explosive qualities than earned him his 'Furia Ceca' moniker.

It didn't start that way for Nedvěd however who, having arrived from Lazio in 2001 in a €41 million move, struggled with the weight of expectation that came with being the man chosen to replace Zinedine Zidane. It was here that his desire, self-motivation and character rose to the fore, putting even greater effort into training sessions and working harder than ever despite things not going well. Eventually he settled in and proved he was simply the most complete midfielder of his generation, a player with no visible weaknesses who was equally capable with both feet. Those skills were enhanced immeasurably by his drive and determination, fuelled by a level of fitness unsurpassed among his fellow professionals.

"I went to a football school 60 miles away from where I lived. I practised twelve hours a day, training both feet so thoroughly that I no longer know which is better. At Sparta Prague, I would retake the field after a match and train until the floodlights were extinguished." – Pavel Nedvěd

Given a nominal role on the left flank, he constantly drifted infield to build attacks, but had the energy to recover and fulfil his defensive duties. During the 2002-03 season, as Juventus marched to their second consecutive title, Nedvěd would enjoy perhaps the greatest period of form in his stellar career. Having eliminated Barcelona, the Bianconeri advanced to face Real Madrid, by now led by Zidane, the very man he had replaced in Turin. The tie was in the balance after Real Madrid's narrow 2-1 victory at the Bernabéu, with David Trezeguet grabbing a precious away goal and leveling the tie within the first twelve minutes of the second leg.

What followed was simply a footballing master class, Nedvěd stealing the show from the Spanish giant's 'Galacticos.' His decisive goal – Juve's third of the game – was just sensational, bettered only by the look on Zidane's face as it hit the back of the net. His fantastic campaign would see him named the winner of the prestigious Balon d'Or as the best player in Europe and also winner of World Soccer's Player of the Year.

Nedvěd could seemingly do everything, constantly making well-timed tackles or interceptions before contributing many varieties up of goal; late arrivals in the box, tap-ins and long range blockbusters. His nineteen-year professional career, which came to an end in 2009, provided an almost endless list of memorable moments across no fewer than 664 appearances, 146 goals, nine league titles and ten cup winners medals. With his good friend Andrea Agnelli taking up the role of President, it was no surprise the former player returned and took up a role on the board of directors, giving the club one more link with its illustrious past.

But it remains Gianluigi Buffon who is perhaps, more than the other four men, the real story here. He had no extended ties to the club like Del Piero, was not coming to the end of his career like Nedvěd and unlike Trezeguet or Camoranesi, was coming to into the peak of his career. Clearly among, if not standing alone as the best player in the world at his position, when the club was relegated he could have had his pick of Europe's top clubs.

He had a similar choice after breaking into the Parma team at a young age, famously repelling countless attacks from the all conquering Milan to keep a clean sheet on his 1995 debut. Buffon went on to play 168 matches in six seasons at the Stadio Tardini, winning an Italian Cup, Italian Super Cup and the UEFA Cup while helping the free spending club to some impressive but ultimately fruitless league title bids.

However, it was still truly shocking to see Juventus pay €45 million for him in 2001 and many thought it excessive as such fees were only being paid for the best attacking talent. The fee remains a world record for a goalkeeper, but 'Superman' has truly fallen in love with La Vecchia Signora and her with him ever since. In Turin he matured quickly, earning global admiration for his leadership, shot stopping ability and the sheer length of time he has been considered among the best keepers in the game.

Countless times Buffon rescued the Bianconeri, stopping shots others simply could not, and he was key in Juve's run in the 2003

Champions League. Stopping a Luis Figo penalty in the semi-final was undoubtedly a highlight and he can be considered unfortunate to have finished on the losing side in that year's final. A string of stunning saves kept the game scoreless, with one from an Inzaghi header evoking memories of Gordon Banks and Pelé at the 1970 World Cup. He would make two more penalty saves as the match went to a shoot-out, but alas it was not meant to be and the Rossoneri eventually triumphed.

At the 2006 World Cup he was similarly excellent, notably making a save from Zinedine Zidane that prevented France from taking the lead. More than anything, it was his leadership that came to the forefront in Germany, his booming voice commanding a constantly changing defence to maintain its shape and deny opponents scoring chances. Conceding a record low of just two goals, the Azzurri managed a 453 minute scoreless streak with a Cristian Zaccardo own-goal and Zidane's penalty in the final book-ending an incredible five clean sheets.

His form was recognised in that year's Balon d'Or voting as he came second to Cannavaro, joining 1963 winner Lev Yashin and 1973 runner-up Dino Zoff as the only keepers ever to be named in the award's top three voting. Buffon began to consider his options that summer, deciding he needed a fresh challenge and all but agreeing a move to Milan. The Calciopoli punishments sparked something in him however and, as he told FourFourTwo magazine in 2008, he realised he must stay with Juventus. He told them:

"Yes, I would have joined Milan, for a new challenge more than anything, but going down to B was challenge enough and I felt that I did the correct thing. Probably it wasn't the normal thing to do but in the end it was a simple choice for me. If Juve had to go down to B then I had to go with them.

"I didn't really need to think about it. Juve helped me become a world champion and therefore I owed them a huge debt. Maybe I had a different upbringing from other players, maybe a different education, especially from my parents in terms of the way I should behave when it came to my dealings with others."

That show of loyalty, rare not just in football, but society in general was so refreshing to see and reminded us – particularly in that darkest of summers – that the beautiful game still has its romantics. His decision to stay endeared him even more to the supporters and cemented his legacy with the club, a fact confirmed on a number of occasions since, when once again the idea of him leaving came to the fore. Much to the relief of Juventini everywhere, he affirmed his affection for the club and renewed his contract, stating his intention to see out his career in Turin.

"Men can go away, executives can go away, but what is really running through this club are the players who have been handed the feel of winning, of being the absolute best, which isn't equalled by any other team." – Gianluigi Buffon, September 2007

Taking over the captaincy from Del Piero and becoming the most capped Italian international of all time have merely added to his legacy and his displays over the past five years have confirmed his place in the pantheon of great Italian keepers at the club. Although heavily interrupted by injury, his performances have seen him join a lineage which began with Gianpiero Combi, flowed through Dino Zoff, Stefano Tacconi and perhaps ended with Angelo Peruzzi.

All have proudly represented both the Azzurri and Juventus. Countless times Buffon has pulled off miracle stops, denying certain goals and winning valuable points for a side which at times has lacked the skill and ability of the man between the posts. Personal accolades have been bestowed with incredible regularity and Buffon, a nine-time winner of the Serie A Goalkeeper of the Year award, has won the International Federation of Football History and Statistics annual honour four times.

The same organisation named him Best Goalkeeper of the 21st Century in February 2012 and, unlike the other four men who endured that season in Serie B, he was once again central to Juve's return to the top under Antonio Conte. Buffon, Camoranesi, Del Piero, Nedvěd and Trezeguet have rightly been awarded places among the fifty legends to be honoured at the inauguration of Juventus Stadium. They will always be held dear by fans of the club, loved not just for staying through Juve's darkest hour, but for their contributions since making that decision.

Legend is a word used all too easily but for these five men, the samurai who pulled on that innocuous looking wristband, it is a most fitting and apt moniker.

THE ALESSIO SECCO
ERROR & BEYOND

Giancarlo Corradini stepped in to lead Juventus in their final two games of the Serie B season. Less than a month later the club appointed Claudio Ranieri as coach for the first year back in the top flight and his arrival, combined with the signings of Vincenzo Iaquinta, Zdeněk Grygera and Portuguese midfielder Tiago, seemed to indicate a club headed in the right direction.

Alessio Secco had been promoted by the new board of directors in the immediate wake of Calciopoli and having worked closely with fellow new arrival Jean-Claude Blanc, the two men had secured financial stability and sponsorship when many of Juve's partners were looking to completely all sever ties with the club. The return to Serie A began brilliantly as the Bianconeri destroyed Livorno 5-1 thanks to a David Trezeguet hat trick. The campaign went well as Juve recorded a revenge-laden 2-1 win over Inter at San Siro and then beat Milan 3-2 to all but ensure a spot in the Champions League at the earliest possible opportunity.

The final game of the season – a 3-3 draw with Sampdoria – saw Del Piero clinch the Serie A scoring title for the first time in his career, narrowly beating strike partner Trezeguet to the Capocannoniere crown. With things certainly on the right track, it was here that Secco started to make the mistakes that would see Juventus begin to struggle rather than thrive and cause damage that would require serious effort to rectify.

Having finished third in the league, the squad required serious improvement in order to challenge the new-found dominance of Inter while competing in the Champions League. Instead, the Sporting Director wasted untold millions on players who were nowhere near the required standard, splashing out on the likes of Amauri and Christian Poulsen during the summer of 2008. The season again started well, with Del Piero netting a stunning free kick in the club's first Champions League game against Zenit St. Petersburg.

The captain would once again take centre stage with three goals in two games against Real Madrid, as his performance at the Bernabéu saw him given a standing ovation by the home supporters, a gesture reserved only for the very best opponents. As great as it was to see the now iconic striker enjoy adding further chapters to his legend, perhaps the two great stories of this post-Calciopoli era are the emergence of Turin native Claudio Marchisio and Giorgio Chiellini as truly top talents.

> *"You live for nights like this and the unique emotion. It is the ultimate feeling in football. To score two goals and win such a big game, then to be applauded by the opposing fans is a sign of recognition that goes beyond rivalry. It was wonderful."*
> *– Alessandro Del Piero on the Stadio Bernabéu*

The latter has become one of the world's best defenders and this could be seen as a result of being bounced around the league in the early part of his career. Having to adapt to a variety of coaches and playing styles, Chiellini is certainly a product of his previous environments. Being brought on as a substitute for Pavel Nedvěd in a home game against Messina in October 2005 would in itself be tough enough, but not for Chiellini. Firstly, Juve were in the midst of a record equalling string of victories. Second, the game was being played out in an almost empty stadium as a protest by Juve fans against the club's policies, with the Ultras only taking to the curva at the interval.

Obviously that summer ended with Juve in Serie B and Chiellini stayed. In a move that would certainly define his role at Juventus, Didier Deschamps would move Chiellini from his usual left-back slot to central defence. He looked more comfortable immediately and began building an outstanding partnership with Nicola Legrottaglie, who he credits with teaching him to play this new role. That pairing would serve Juve upon returning to Serie A and during that season another uncompromising first impression of Chiellini would come for British fans, probably seeing him for the first time at the opening match of the new Wembley Stadium. Playing for Italy's Under 21 side, he received an accidental kick to the head but the captain played on, bloodstained and bandaged, but still winning headers.

2008 was another busy year for Chiellini, being fundamental in the club's pursuit of Champions League football. An inspired performance against Inter at San Siro saw him close to fighting with Ibrahimović while keeping the Swede at bay throughout the game. He also scored two goals in a 5-2 demolition of Lazio, while later that same summer his uncompromising style would raise its head again. A fully committed challenge in training would see him put captain Fabio Cannavaro out for the Euro 2008 tournament. Undaunted, the Juve man filled his spot brilliantly, in particular against Fernando Torres and Spain in the quarter-final.

Chiellini's qualities saw him named Serie A's best defender for three straight seasons. His tough style echoes that of Claudio Gentile, but – in a complete paradox – he exudes a fairness and honesty that is reminiscent of the great Gaetano Scirea. An embodiment of the Juve spirit, fans were proud to see him captain the side when Del Piero or Buffon were unavailable, an honour which also occasionally falls to his teammate Marchisio.

The young midfielder also burst into the team during the season in Serie B when, unsure of when they would see their beloved Bianconeri back among the elite of European football, the club's fans consoled themselves with the fact their team would now be filled with promising young Italian players turned out year after year by one of the country's most successful youth systems. Under the previous regime, these players were all too often destined to spend their years being loaned around the league or be used as leverage in deals for players who could help win trophies now rather than later. This was the Juventus of Luciano Moggi, who only aimed to win in the here and now – to them the future may as well have been on another planet.

Even with that management team gone, Marchisio had to fight for his place with a number of more famous, not to mention expensive, imports as Juve sought to return to glory. He rose to the challenge, becoming a first team regular despite the presence of Cristiano Zanetti and later Tiago, Momo Sissoko and Christian Poulsen. He was even named Serie A Player of the Month for December 2008 after a string of impressive displays, including a winning goal against Inter in the Derby d'Italia.

However, Marchisio is not without his critics. He is often accused of inconsistent and indifferent performances and has been described as 'invisible' on a number of occasions. Yet to people who see past the match highlights and score-sheet, the midfielder has actually become a key player in many different ways. He can of course win matches – that much has been made clear as he has netted vital goals against Italy's biggest sides – but he can also be deployed in various roles. His intelligence and positional awareness nullify the opposition's better players in a manner that is all but impossible to measure using statistics or gauge by watching television.

Even with these two becoming pillars of the side, the team would crash out of the Champions League against Chelsea in February of 2009. Then, following a 4-1 win away to Roma, the team would collapse and record six draws and a loss that would bring Ranieri's tenure to an end. Ciro Ferrara was appointed caretaker coach and won the final two games to clinch second place some ten points behind champions Inter. Ranieri deserved better and it was a clear case of the club management blaming the coach for what was ultimately a deeply flawed squad.

The following summer saw even more questionable decisions as Fabio Cannavaro, one of the players to flee as the Calciopoli scandal broke, returned from Real Madrid. A move always likely to stir emotions, the Ultras – perhaps already appeased somewhat by his status as a national hero following the 2006 World Cup – then appeared to 'forgive' him after he bought pizza for their leaders. Whilst morally questionable, from a footballing point of view the transfer did make some sense as bringing in an international class defender for no fee provided experience and guidance to young stoppers like Cristian Molinaro and Paolo De Ceglie. Adding some much needed creativity and spark to a previously dull midfield was essential, and acquiring Brazilian player, Diego, filled a gap created by the retirement of Pavel Nedvěd.

The move was also struck early in the summer, giving the player and club time to learn how to get the best from each other while walking away from a potential banana skin in Udine when the asking price for Gaetano D'Agostino continued to rise. To follow that move with a proven Serie A talent in Felipe Melo was also impressive. The loan signing of Martin Cáceres gave Ferrara – now given the job on a permanent basis – a chance to see if he could cope with Italian football, before investing serious money.

A seemingly promising start, the new signings left the job half done. Juventus clearly needed fullbacks to help provide width in Ferrara's 4-3-1-2 formation, but none came close to arriving. To outsiders it appeared the man who replaced Moggi had finally grasped what was required of him, but anyone taking more than a passing glance could see the ever-increasing flaws. For all his predecessors many errors, Moggi always provided answers and ensured his coach always had the players he required. In this Secco era, Juve had at least as many problems as they did solutions, but as Napoleon famously said, "much more is learned from defeat than there ever is from winning."

Ciro Ferrara, hugely inexperienced as coach, was sacked after just four months in charge as results began to go against him. An embarrassing 4-1 defeat to Bayern Munich eliminated Juventus from the Champions League and all but sealed his fate. Then, Alberto

Zaccheroni was brought in, but after an initial improvement results and performances were as bad as they ever were under Ferrara. Another humiliating 4-1 loss – this time to Fulham – saw the club out of Europe all together and they eventually finished in seventh place after losing an incredible fifteen matches.

They conceded more goals than they actually scored, with the club's top scorer – Del Piero – netting just nine times. The Bianconeri suffered not one, but two embarrassing exits from Europe and sacked two coaches in what was about as far from a vintage year it was possible to get. This Juventus were, frankly, a disgraceful shadow of the greatness with which La Vecchia Signora had become synonymous. Following the logic of the French Emperor, the club must be the most intelligent in Italy. As the knowledge gained in a season of adversity like that would help in the plans for the future; it immediately had some wide-reaching effects.

Blanc and Secco were viewed as one entity by fans tired of seeing their great club tarnished by such poor performances, but giving them an equal share of the blame was unfair given their clearly defined roles at the club. Blanc was the Chairman, responsible for the day-to-day and long-term running of the huge business that is Juventus Football Club. During his tenure Juventus recovered from relegation, began building a new stadium, provided huge funds for both wages and transfers and still managed to be one of the only big European clubs to turn a substantial profit.

In terms of finance, business and infrastructure, he was a visionary leader, identifying various problems and finding unique and brilliant solutions. Descriptions of him often see him painted as a 'French businessman' and that was his biggest problem. He never fully understood what Juventus means to those who truly cherish the Bianconeri colours, but he was clearly not – and never claimed to be – a 'football man.' Secco was the sporting director, responsible for the football operation, appointing coaches, signing players and transfers.

Previous chairman Giovanni Coboli-Gigli appointed him to the position in 2006 and after Blanc took command, he gave Secco one transfer window – the summer of 2009 – to prove himself. Obviously by the winter break the errors were glaring and he acted swiftly. Two problem players – Tiago and Cristian Molinaro – were sent out on loan and a coaching change was made. By bringing back Roberto Bettega and removing much of the power and influence from Secco, Blanc immediately resolving a number of issues. Antonio Candreva was brought in to offer width and invention to a midfield seriously lacking both qualities. All were necessary moves made by Bettega and all issues that could, and should, have been seen by the sporting director the previous summer.

What Juventus needed was a new figurehead, a leader, someone the fans could look to and believe in, knowing the future of their club is safe. A President needed to be appointed, a man who the supporters would not question, one who can invoke the spirit of Juventus that was so obviously missing. After a year in the purgatory of Serie B, followed by three seasons of relative mediocrity, the name Agnelli would once again be placed on the door to the President's office at Italy's most famous club.

This move, coupled with Secco's forced resignation and a largely reduced role for Blanc, was a clear statement of intent, to the Italian Football Association, the FIGC, and the rest of the league that Juventus intend to reclaim their place atop Serie A. Andrea Agnelli's appointment heralded, if not a bright new start, then a desire to recapture old glories. It meant that a man with Juventus in his heart, and indeed his blood, was back in the seat of power. It also shows that the long overdue revolution had begun in earnest.

"Juve were having issues recovering from the events of 2006
so we decided we needed a family member in charge."
– Andrea Agnelli on becoming President

During the interview in which he revealed the appointment, Andrea's cousin and FIAT Chairman, John Elkann revealed just how valuable the return of the family name was to the club. He also promised that the club would ask for the 2005-06 Scudetto – awarded to Inter following Calciopoli – be revoked, asking for fair and equal treatment for all clubs. He was very careful not to deny guilt, merely asking everyone to receive the same punishment, as clearly every club was doing the same things as Luciano Moggi. Elkann also acknowledged the stellar financial work done by Blanc and added that the move would enable him to concentrate on the aspects of the business in which he excels.

Beppe Marotta was appointed as Director General, bringing with him an incredible knowledge of the game and the transfer market. This immediately provided the club the much needed leadership and direction it had sorely lacked over the previous four seasons. Sadly, however, their arrival heralded the need to trim significant sums from the wage budget and also coincided with one of the club's heroes expressing a desire to leave. Juventus fans will always appreciate the man known simply as 'Trezegol' but leaving when he did was an arrangement that suited both parties. It drew to an end a ten-year spell with the Bianconeri, one that will always be remembered for his amazing goal-scoring prowess.

The search for a striker of Trezeguet's ability is one area where Marotta seemingly failed. Yet his more immediate issue concerned finding the right coach. Ciro Ferrara was found to be too inexperienced while Alberto Zaccheroni experimented – both with players and tactics – far too often. The ideal solution was to bring in a man with fixed ideas and a wealth of experience. After it seemed that Rafael Benitez would be that man, the new regime wisely decided to stick to those schooled in the Italian game. Not only was Gigi Delneri all these things, he was also well known to Marotta having worked under him at Sampdoria.

While his career had made stops in Chievo, Palermo and Atalanta, Delneri had also tasted the big club atmosphere at Roma and Porto. That experience, allied to a provincial mentality, has always been part of Juve's unique make-up. Unfortunately, Delneri would eventually prove to have far too much of the latter. After his new look team began the season in great form, even managing to look like title contenders going into the winter break, the 2010-11 season would end with him and the players looking bewildered. The coach became deeply disliked by the majority of supporters and looked ever more out of his depth.

The club lost ten games, conceding almost as many goals as they scored and ended the campaign in seventh place yet again. This disappointment meant the Bianconeri would be absent from Europe altogether the following season. That realisation only compounded what had already been a savagely inadequate campaign. Juventus failed to advance from the group stage of the Europa League and were eliminated from the Coppa Italia in a disappointing quarter-final display against Roma. Delneri's Juventus were a failure almost any way you judged them. Yet, as he has throughout his career, Delneri accepted responsibility for his mistakes and the man himself informed the audience of reporters at a training ground press conference that his time in Turin had come to an end.

His departure was inevitable as fans continued similar protests to those that marred the short and ill-fated tenure of Zaccheroni just twelve months previously. The malaise and depressed air that permeated into almost every facet of Italian football's grand Old Lady could continue no longer. Marotta, along with the club President, made what the former described as a "sad, difficult but ultimately necessary decision" in an interview with La Stampa. Delneri's mindset and understanding of what it took to hold such a prestigious role was obviously questioned, but the same could not be said of the man who would replace him.

Perhaps the biggest event that season, however, was that Milan secured the Serie A title. Ignoring the continued legal wrangling and politics which continue to rage, looking from a purely footballing perspective, seeing a team other than Inter winning the title drew a neat line under that particular era. While nothing should ever detract from the amazing achievements of Jose Mourinho's treble-winning Inter, it is equally nonsensical to deny the advantages afforded to the Nerazzurri in the immediate aftermath of the original Calciopoli.

As the verdicts of the original trial rocked Serie A to its very core, it was described by many as something of a 'year zero' for Italian football, but in truth it never was. With a previously dominant Juventus first stripped of so many top players and their entire management structure, then sent to Serie B while Milan, Fiorentina and Lazio started with negative points totals, it was more like one million years B.C. It gave birth to a feeling that the real race could now begin from a starting point at which all the competitors were on an equal footing, a starting point Juventus would seize full advantage of...

A NEW DAWN BRINGS AN UNBEATEN RUN

"The dark years of finishing in seventh place were much worse than Calciopoli and being demoted to Serie B. To get right back up and in fact win the title unbeaten will always remain in the history of Juventus. It was unique and special."
– Giorgio Chiellini

Sometimes, even those who have watched football for years can still be shocked by events in the game, so much so that it makes them once again fall in love with the sport in the way they first did as a child. Following a dire two years at the club, which under the guidance of Ciro Ferrara, Alberto Zaccheroni and Gigi Delneri, had yielded consecutive seventh place finishes, the club management decided widespread changes were needed. As they have so many times previously, Juventus chose to delve into her past in order to secure a brighter future.

Shortly before the 2010-11 season drew to a close, Beppe Marotta announced the departure of the moustachioed Delneri – a close personal friend of the Director General – and unveiled none other than Antonio Conte as his replacement. The new coach had, of course, captained the club during Marcello Lippi's first highly successful stint at Juventus, but had very limited managerial experience which, aside from a poor nineteen game spell in charge of Atalanta, had been gained exclusively outside of the peninsula's top division.

As well as bringing in a man whose biggest coaching accomplishments were guiding both Siena and Bari out of Serie B, the club once again failed to deliver the big name striker long promised by Marotta. Instead, he had brought in a number of players who had been solid, if unspectacular, at their previous clubs, as Stephan Lichtsteiner came from Lazio and Arturo Vidal was brought over from Germany. While capable of brilliance, fans also rightly questioned the wisdom in acquiring the hugely inconsistent Mirko Vučinić from Roma.

However, the main area of concern was Conte, a man whose grasp of the famous Juventus spirit could never be questioned. He also appeared to share a number of flaws with Delneri as the 4-2-4 formation so beloved by Conte since he swapped the armband for the bench was also championed by his predecessor. It was a set-up which had served him well in the lower leagues, but one which was deemed wholly unsuitable for the demands of top flight football as many observers realised it would be quickly overrun in midfield.

Yet those doubts – and many others besides – would be allayed on the opening day of the campaign by a man who would announce his arrival in a manner similar to the way he first entered into the public eye over a decade earlier. An April day in 2001 would bear witness to a midfielder coming of age as Roberto Baggio controlled a long, dropping ball with a typically divine touch, floating past Edwin van der Sar before sending the ball into the back of the empty goal. It helped lowly Brescia to earn a point away to a heavily favoured Juventus, but the goal and, more significantly, the incredible pass which led to it, announced the arrival of Andrea Pirlo as a deep-lying midfield play-maker to a wider audience.

While many in his native Italy may well have been fully aware of the then 21 year old, it was in a very different guise to the one on display that afternoon at the Stadio delle Alpi in Turin. Gone was the traditional number ten who had played just behind the strikers in a career which already spanned some six years and included spells at Inter and Reggina. In that advanced position he had also played a starring role at the European Under-21 Championships in 2000 where he was captain, player of the tournament and top scorer for a victorious Italy side.

Here was a player wearing the number five shirt and sitting just in front of the defence, yet rather than offering protection like a typical defensive midfielder, he instead controlled the game, set the tempo and distributed the ball, reinvented in a role which many considered long since forgotten. Luckily for Pirlo, and subsequently Milan, Juventus and the national team, his coach at Brescia, Carlo Mazzone, had been around long enough to remember the days that such players regularly ran the show. In some ways the move was forced upon both men, the presence of Baggio meaning Pirlo's usual berth was occupied and a new position needed to be found.

The insight and belief shown by Carlo Ancelotti in taking Pirlo and deploying him in the 'regista' role at Milan should also be applauded. It was a leap of faith which, while not as inspired or original as when Mazzone first made the switch, was never the less just as vital to the emergence of the player we know today. Since those early games in Lombardia, the footballing world could not fail to notice his development as he matured from being Baggio's young apprentice into a thoroughly accomplished midfielder.

Growing in stature by the year, Pirlo went on to set the tone for two Champions League wins with the San Siro outfit, as well as Italy's 2006 World Cup win. That tournament in Germany, perhaps more than any other period in his career, marked him out as one of this generation's true greats as he played better than ever. He even managed to break the Azzurri tradition of starting World Cups slowly as he scored a wonderful long range goal in their opening game, a 2-0 win over Ghana where he was named man of the match. He would win the same accolade in the epic semi-final victory over the hosts as well as the final when he was once again brilliant, a performance often forgotten amid the drama of the penalty shoot-out and Zinedine Zidane's shocking dismissal.

Five years later, along the way having inspired Milan's revenge over Liverpool in the 2007 Champions League Final, it still came as something of a surprise when, despite a couple of injury-hit seasons, the Rossoneri chose not to offer him a new contract. The decision was taken by Milan Vice-President Adriano Galliani after listening to both the advice of Jean-Pierre Meersemann, head of the clubs famous MilanLab medical facility, and coach Massimiliano Allegri. Having seen Roberto Donadoni's Italy eliminated from Euro 2008 by Spain when a suspended Pirlo missed the quarter-final and Marcello Lippi being utterly humiliated at the 2010 World Cup where injury restricted the midfielder to a mere 34-minute cameo in the third group game, Allegri's opinion carried much weight as he became perhaps the first coach to find a way to win without Pirlo.

During Milan's run to the Scudetto in 2010-11 the player managed just twelve starts, his lowest total since his first season at San Siro and usually found himself stuck out on the left side of midfield as his new coach looked to reinvigorate that area of the team. Abandoning the inventiveness and creativity of Pirlo in favour of more traditional stoppers like Marc van Bommel and the energy of Kevin-Prince Boateng Milan had, in the words of Barcelona coach Pep Guardiola, "lost a fantastic player".

Few believed that, at the highest level at least, the midfielder was still capable of being as important as Guardiola, who actually replaced Pirlo at Brescia when he moved to Milan, still believed him to be. Pirlo smiled as Galliani gave him a pen, an engraved Cartier embossed with the Milan club logo that perhaps made the perfect gift for a long time supporter of the *Rossoneri*. But for a player who is possibly the greatest Italian midfielder of all time, Andrea Pirlo felt that after so many years in those famous red and black stripes, he deserved so much more. "It was a lovely pen, but still a pen. Filled with banal blue ink", he wrote in his recent autobiography, *Penso Quindi Gioco* ("I think, therefore I play"). "Adriano Galliani told me, 'Make sure you don't use that to sign a new contract with Juventus'". Unfortunately for the Milan Vice-President and all connected with the club, the Flero native would do just that.

"As a goodbye gift I expected something more than that perfect comic timing. My ten years of Milan, gone like that. I smiled anyway", Pirlo wrote – although probably not with that same pen. After a decade of seeing him as a rival, fans of the Bianconeri would embrace the midfielder who would look immediately at home in Turin. In his first game, he would be utterly dominant in a way he hadn't been in the entire previous campaign

That debut was also the opening game of Conte's tenure and it would perfectly encapsulate everything that Juventus would become over the next forty-eight matches, beginning a number of narratives that would continue to run even when the team finally tasted defeat. It would also mark the first game at the brand new Juventus Stadium, as Parma became the first competitive opponents to face La Madama in her new home. Led by Turin native and Juve youth product Sebastian Giovinco – at that point co-owned by the two sides – the Ducali had twice beaten Delneri's team in the previous campaign and the stark difference in 2011-12 would quickly become evident.

The match had seen just fifteen minutes of play when, having had his own route to goal blocked by not one but two opposing players, Pirlo checked his run and almost without looking clipped a ball over the top of the static Parma back line. Just like his ball to Roberto Baggio ten years earlier, it floated perfectly and dropped to the feet of Lichtsteiner who had cut in unnoticed from his position on the right. The Swiss full-back controlled the ball with one foot before slotting past the helpless Antonio Mirante with the other, the ball soon nestling into the back of the visitors goal. Their new home had its first competitive strike and Juventus had not only found a new hero, but Italy would rediscover the undeniable genius of Andrea Pirlo.

Conte had done more than simply make room for Pirlo, he had followed the lead of Mazzone, Ancelotti and Lippi by making his newest acquisition the focal point of the side where he could once again live up to his nickname, "The Architect". Flanked by willing runners like Arturo Vidal, Claudio Marchisio and Simone Pepe, it worked wonderfully from that very first day in a manner unthinkable even to the most ardent of fans.

Eventually running out 4-1 winners, Juventus would – despite not recording the second goal until midway through the second half – exert their dominance through that same irresistible mixture of confident and assured passing and relentless pressing discussed previously. Parma would be out-tackled and Juventus would intercept the ball countless times, restricting the hapless Gialloblu to less than 30% possession as they pushed home their advantage, completing 400 more passes than their well-beaten opponents.

In what would become a weekly occurrence, Pirlo was at the heart of everything they did that day, amassing 122 touches of the ball, almost all of which became passes to a team-mate, adding a second assist as the Bianconeri completed their first rout of the season. Pirlo created two goals and completed a remarkable 110 passes, much to the delight of Gigi Buffon who told *La Repubblica*; "It's the bargain of the century for us. Seeing him play in front of my back line, it made me realise that God does exist."

He carried that form through the entire campaign registering three goals, thirteen assists and, perhaps more tellingly, created over 100 clear scoring opportunities for a team which has sadly wasted so many of those chances. He completed more passes than any other player in Serie A, yet to reduce a player of such ability to mere statistics is to strip away everything which makes him great; the style, grace and effortless nature which define not only his playing style but also the man himself. Often spoken of as the one true champion in a young and hungry Juventus squad, he is exactly as Lippi famously described him when he said; "Pirlo is a silent leader. He speaks with his feet."

Those same feet were praised back in 2007 by another iconic figure, the man perhaps most responsible for the Barcelona we see today, a team which embraces the same characteristics seen in the Italians play. As Johan Cruyff told the press at a UEFA conference "Pirlo can make his feet do whatever he wants. He's a genius." Watching him stroke the ball around with consummate ease, even under the heaviest pressure it is hard to argue with such an assessment and seeing him use his ability to read the game to both set up team-mates and disrupt the play of opponents is to witness a once-a-generation level of talent.

That he is held in such esteem by the Dutch maestro is very telling, as the player seems to thrive under those who know what the game is like after playing similar roles themselves. It is no secret Ancelotti won back-to-back European Cups at the heart of those incredible Milan teams of the late 1980s and early '90s, while even Lippi enjoyed a modest playing career in Sampdoria's midfield. Perhaps then Conte's past as a Champions League winning midfielder is his greatest asset when dealing with Pirlo, surely giving him insight and understanding what his new charge needs in order to be at his best.

The belief that La Madama would shine if her newest leading man was allowed the freedom to excel was stated most pointedly by a man who knew something about delivering silverware to Turin's Old Lady. Michel Platini, the man Bianconeri fans dubbed 'The King', told La Stampa that "if Pirlo is on song, everything else falls into place." That was true back in 2001 when his assist to Baggio took the title away from Juventus and into the hands of that year's eventual champion Roma, and it remained so as history came full circle. Now he was the one wearing the famous black and white stripes and his new club found those incredible passes could lead them back to the promised land.

If the first goal against Parma was a sign of things to come, the second highlighted a rare on-field contribution from a man who became more beloved for his antics away from the pitch. It would be scored by Simone Pepe, a player who clung to the touchline and wore his hair short, closely cropped hair in a style more military than modern. Shunning the unnecessary preening, posturing and posing shown by many of his contemporaries, the former Palermo man was something of a throw-back to a bygone era. Far from certain of a starting berth, his attitude, application and ability would see him become vital to Juventus, despite the fact his signing was met with cries of derision from the majority of fans.

One of the first acquisitions of the new Andrea Agnelli-led regime, there were many all-too-fresh memories of Pepe's frankly abject performances at the earlier World Cup in South Africa. There he cut an isolated form in an ill-fitting and incompatible midfield that failed comprehensively to display any unity, cohesion or understanding.

Yet in the intervening seven months, through a combination of the very qualities found in his illustrious predecessor Angelo Di Livio, Pepe has won over all but the most stubborn-minded tifosi. Cutting a figure remarkably similar to the Lippi-era winger, many had a complete 180 degree turn-around of opinion, now loving a man they loathed upon hearing of his capture. Even more than this versatility, his most telling impact has been his sense of humour and ability to improve camaraderie, priceless commodities in the high pressure atmosphere which always surrounds the Old Lady.

Following on from that opening day victory, all those questions, those doubts which plagued even the most ardent of the club's fans, were quashed by a team who steamrollered all before them, and they did so while accomplishing something almost no Juve side had ever managed to do. Neutral fans – if such a thing exists where this most divisive of clubs is concerned – actually enjoyed seeing them succeed. As difficult as it was to comprehend, the once-loathed Bianconeri were gaining admirers both at home and abroad thanks to a thoroughly modern style of play.

Conte eventually adopted what was essentially a 3-5-2 formation after twice changing his basic framework in his debut campaign on the Juve bench. He first abandoned the 4-2-4 to accommodate Arturo Vidal and Andrea Pirlo alongside Claudio Marchisio in midfield then shelved the 4-3-3 alternative due to the lack of belief in wingers Miloš Krasić and Eljero Elia. For all their aesthetic beauty, it was tempered by a contradiction so typical of Juventus, as they became a cohesive and devastating defensive unit.

They pressed the ball in a manner which carried huge echoes of Conte's playing days as they showcased a relentless desire to win back the ball as quickly as possible, bringing a style not seen in Italy since the halcyon days of Arrigo Sacchi's Milan. The coach instilled an appetite and hunger in the team which made not conceding space and time one of their fundamental values and made life exceptionally difficult for each and every opponent they faced.

It seemed almost laughable that less than a year earlier many were sceptical of Conte's appointment, wondering how he would rise to the challenge of leading one of European football's truly giant clubs, and how his beloved 4-2-4 would cope with the complexities of one of the most tactically astute leagues in the world. Simply put, he passed with flying colours. Instilling his players a belief that they were always good enough to clinch victory and a desire to never lose, Conte abandoned his trademark formation almost before the season began and it made no difference which framework he formed his squad around. Every single week the players gave their all to ensure Conte's orders were carried out.

Chiellini would ensure few attacks would enjoy success down the left, while another Italy international would ensure their opponents would have little chance to answer Juve's devastating attack on the right flank. Slowly but surely, Andrea Barzagli began to earn his place among the most respected defenders in the world, but in order to understand just how great he had become, it was important to know his journey to Turin, to see what made him the player he is today.

His career began with fourth-tier club Rondinella back in 1998. From there he bounced around the lower divisions until finally making his Serie A debut with exciting newcomers Chievo in 2003. Twelve months later he moved again, this time to Palermo, where he would establish himself as an above-average defender and an infrequent member of the Italy squad. Barzagli would go to the 2006 World Cup as the fourth-choice centre-back, but injury to Alessandro Nesta and the suspension of Marco Materazzi saw him earn vital playing time.

He was superb when coming on as a substitute against Australia, but was rarely tested in the quarter-final against Ukraine before returning to the bench. Two more average seasons in Sicily would follow before Euro 2008 came around. Injury to Fabio Cannavaro meant he was chosen to partner Materazzi in the opening game against the Netherlands and it would prove to be a disaster. The Azzurri were swept aside 3-0 and Barzagli's performance was so poor he would make just one substitute appearance for Italy over the following three seasons.

Just days later, a shocking move to Wolfsburg was announced with the Bundesliga outfit grossly overpaying for his services. Despite winning the league title in his debut campaign, he never looked like an €11 million defender during his time in Germany and the following season the side would be limping to an eighth-place finish with Barzagli eventually losing his place in the side and being sold to Juventus for just €300,000. His first six months saw him make little impact on an already doomed Bianconeri, themselves struggling to a second successive disappointing season. Perhaps no reputation has improved as much under Conte's guidance than Barzagli, who turned in consistently flawless performances for club and country once Gigi Delneri was replaced.

Alongside Chiellini, his commanding performances saw him nicknamed "La Roccia" and he is undoubtedly the rock on which the current Juventus defence is built. While his arrival for almost no fee would turn out to be one of the best transfers of Marotta's tenure, the third member of Conte's back three was initially greeted with immense scepticism. When Juventus announced the €15 million signing of Leonardo Bonucci from Genoa in the summer of 2009, it looked like they had, despite the arrival of a new and supposedly more astute management team, once again overspent on a player. His early showings in the Bianconeri shirt did little to appease those fears among supporters who had seen defenders such as Jorge Andrade, Jean-Alain Boumsong and the disastrous return of an ageing Fabio Cannavaro all flop in recent years.

The perception was that, once again, the club had failed to find a solid addition for the back-line and brought in yet another player unfit to follow in the footsteps of names as illustrious as Gaetano Scirea, Ciro Ferrara and Lilian Thuram. There were even those who believed Marotta had signed the wrong member of a relatively successful Bari side, instead lamenting that Andrea Ranocchia wasn't the one brought to Turin. With Bari he always appeared to be the lesser of the pair, despite being the one with links to a bigger club.

Cut loose by Inter as part of the deal that brought Thiago Motta and Diego Milito to the Giuseppe Meazza, Bonucci began to attract attention as he helped the Southern club improve upon Antonio Conte's excellent promotion the season before. In his first season in Turin he made countless mistakes costing a number of points yet to some – largely those who remembered the similarly difficult early days of some truly great defenders – there were, even in those early days, signs that Bonucci could one day become one himself.

To those who took time to look closely enough, he clearly possessed all the tools necessary to succeed. Physically, he was already an imposing figure as the unfortunate soul who tried to steal his watch a year or two later would discover. One problem Bonucci and other defenders must always overcome is the intricacies of a new system and, thanks to Conte, he has been blessed in Turin to have had coaches who pay attention to every detail.

New to playing in a three man back-line, he adapted well, quickly learning what position on the field to take up and where his team-mates should be, when to move and where to be as well as who was responsible for which opposition player. While it often looks effortless during matches, knowing those factors is the result of hours of hard work on the training ground from all involved and the understanding between the players on the pitch was a huge factor in Bonucci's improvement under Conte.

His passing was also better following the dismissal of Delneri as he was often given time on the ball rarely afforded to defenders. He utilised that space well, and Bonucci often took on the burden of the playmaking duties when Pirlo was well-marked. Occasionally completing more passes than the iconic midfielder, he was often central in leading the team to celebrate wins under the stands and cemented his place in supporters hearts in February 2012. Suspended for the visit of Fiorentina, he chose to take a seat with the fans in the Curva Sud rather than wear a suit and sit behind the bench. Clips of him wildly cheering the side's two goals and joining in with chants earned him huge admiration among fans as they spread across the internet.

With the trio regularly swapping the black and white stripes for the blue shirt of Italy, Bonucci became central to both club and country alongside Barzagli and Chiellini, maturing into a fine defender and a key figure in the success of the three-man backline. When it came to this Juventus, never was the old maxim that defence wins championships more appropriate. Thanks to their impressive play, the Bianconeri were positively miserly, not only conceding just nineteen goals, but allowing a meagre 9.2 shots per game a total again only bettered on the continent by Bayern Munich and Barcelona. Gigi Buffon was reduced to watching in most games, making just 79 saves on his way to a jaw-dropping 21 clean sheets.

One criticism of the team was the lack of a regular goal-scorer, and with no fewer than fifteen other Serie A players topping Alessandro Matri's team high of ten goals, it was perhaps something of a concern. However, no less than eighteen different players found the back of the net during the campaign. With five of those registering at least six goals, Juventus lead the way with 46 strikes from open play for yet another league best, with only Milan scoring more total goals.

Team after team would fall by the wayside, perhaps most notably in a six-week spell during March and April which began with a 5-0 thrashing of Fiorentina in Tuscany followed by wins over Inter, Napoli, Palermo, Lazio and Roma. In those five games, Juve outscored their rivals by eighteen goals to one to secure their grasp on a first Serie A crown since the pre-Calciopoli era.

They would steamroller their way through the entire campaign without losing a single league game, an unthinkable accomplishment after the two woeful seventh-place finishes which preceded the arrival of Antonio Conte, and the undefeated streak was almost entirely due to the man on the bench. The galvanising effect of his appointment carried them through the early weeks of 2011-12 and his dedicated and detailed approach to his new role sustained them once it became a realistic goal. When games were close or difficult, he was always ready with a wise word, a smart substitution or a refreshing team selection that sharpened the team's focus and drove them on to further greatness in the seasons to follow.

CONTE CONTINUES & HISTORY IS REWRITTEN

"Solo chi vince scrive la storia" – "Only winners write history"
– Antonio Conte

In lifting their first league title of the post-Calciopoli era, Antonio Conte had ensured that in just over twelve months in charge he had revitalised Juventus, helping the Old Lady rediscover her desire for victory. Overhauling almost every facet of the club, he had quickly reminded everyone of that famous Juventus spirit, that anything other than winning was, in essence, failure.

His relentless drive and motivation was constantly on the verge of maniacal, an obsessive winner who simply refused to accept defeat. The Scudetto would be sealed in a match in Trieste against Cagliari and then a joyous afternoon at Juventus Stadium against Atalanta the following week saw them presented with the trophy. That would see the sad end of Alessandro Del Piero's time in Turin however, with the club confirming their tearful captain would no longer be pulling on the famous black and white stripes.

In a strange paradox, it would be helpful to the coach that his undefeated Bianconeri would ultimately still end 2011-12 as losers. Having eliminated Roma and Milan en route to the Italian Cup Final, Conte's men would be thoroughly outplayed in the showpiece event by Napoli, seeing their perfect season tarnished in its very last match. They would take that defeat personally, beating the same opponents in August's Super Coppa curtain raiser before marching into their second campaign the way they had finished the first one.

It would be a season that would begin in odd circumstances however, with Conte and assistant coach Angelo Alessio banned for their alleged failure to report a fixed match whilst still at Siena. Even that would fail to slow this incredible side even slightly and Technical Director Massimo Carrera would lead the team impressively in the absence of the pair, relinquishing control to Alessio who returned slightly ahead of his boss.

Between this unorthodox trio, Juventus would march impressively to the 2012-13 winter break eight points clear atop the Serie A table, qualifying for the quarter-finals of both the Italian Cup and the

Champions League thanks to that same heady blend of passing, pressing and belief which had served them so well throughout the previous campaign. But Conte was understandably far from happy at the situation, launching into a tirade at a press conference shortly before he was banned.

"I think", he told reporters, "that credibility is something you earn every day and I think that throughout my life, I have gained great credibility. Unlike those who have sold matches, sold themselves, their families and their team-mates for the past three years!" Those words, the first among many others, formed part of a lengthy press conference shortly after his first appeal against the ten-month suspension handed to him that summer. It was a hearing that dismissed one charge against Conte and upheld another, but failed to deliver any reduction in sentence meaning the reigning Serie A champions would effectively be without their leader for the entire campaign.

Just over a month later and the Italian Olympic Committee would cut the punishment to just four months for one count of "failure to report" an allegedly fixed match while he was in charge of Siena during the 2010-11 campaign. However, even before the original punishment was handed down, Juventus had chosen to install Carrera as stand-in coach meaning Conte had effectively started his ban before any judgment was made.

"I see a caged lion", Gianluigi Buffon said as he saw how his coach was coping with being removed from active duty. The goalkeeper added that "It's not like Conte's suspension is helping the team, a coach like him influences in the same way in the changing room and from the bench during the game." However, looking from the outside, the ban seemed to have hardly affected the side at all.

They sat top of Serie A, two points clear of the chasing pack and, despite the end of the remarkable 49-match unbeaten run, dropped points in just four league games. Carrera led them to silverware in the Italian Super Cup, dispatching Napoli in an ill-tempered affair before assistant Angelo Alessio, himself banned for the same incident as Conte, returned. He in turn guided them to the top of a Champions League group that included not only Shakhtar Donetsk – a tough proposition for any team – but also holders Chelsea, soundly beaten in Turin.

In total, Conte's ban spanned 21 official fixtures with Juve winning fourteen, drawing five and losing just two – to Milan and Inter. Yet for those close to the club, living its day to day reality, even having Conte available for training during the week is a world away from having him there on the touchline. "He yells at us a lot", Claudio Marchisio said during the ban, "gesticulating with both passion and purpose, striving to make his team the very best they can be." Just as obvious to most observers is that this is most certainly a team created in his image and bending to his will, as he drags every ounce of effort and ability from his players in the same way he once did when patrolling the midfield for Marcello Lippi's dominant Juve sides of the nineties.

"We miss Conte a lot, especially at half-time", Andrea Pirlo revealed that October, adding that "he has the right words for everyone and can change the outcome of a game with his tactical adjustments." Those sentiments have been echoed by almost everyone at the club, perhaps none more so than Giorgio Chiellini, who told reporters at a press conference in early November: "He is the person who has changed the team over the past year and a half. I initially thought his absence would be less problematic, but there are things that you cannot plan for and the coach is important in certain situations. His return to the bench will give the team a boost."

They were paired with a marauding Bayern Munich in the quarter-final of the Champions League and the German side beat them handily by four goals over two legs. It never once felt like a real contest and that loss, coupled with a Coppa Italia exit at the hands of Vladimir Petković's impressive Lazio side, would spur the Bianconeri on to seal their second consecutive Scudetto at a canter. Reeling off nine consecutive league wins, the confetti and silverware were once again proudly on show in a wonderful Turin celebration.

However, the crushing loss to Germany's super club burned just as the previous loss to Napoli had a year earlier, leaving the same indelible mark on all those of a Bianconeri persuasion which would drive them to improve further still. Speaking at an end of season event to celebrate their second successive league title there were some telling words from Andrea Agnelli, the president hinting at what lay ahead as he told those present:

"Juventus taught me one thing above all else, which is that the best triumph is the one still to come. That is why I am already concentrated on next season, because Juve haven't won a third consecutive Scudetto since the five in a row of the 1930s. This is a new great motivation."

During the pre-season build up, Conte too spoke at length about the possibility of doing what neither Marcello Lippi nor Giovanni Trapattoni had managed at their peak and win three league titles in a row. To continue their progression in Europe was also important to all concerned, but it was clear that the coach's primary focus was on the domestic front. While Conte talked of creating history, questions were asked about whether Juve would be motivated for another gruelling campaign as Napoli, Fiorentina and Roma had all strengthened immeasurably in order to catch La Madama.

At their pre-season retreat however, it would be another figure who would take charge, a role he had taken on almost two years previously and one he had yet to relinquish. There, high in the Aostan hills, it didn't take onlookers long to recognise the coach leading the Juventus squad through a punishing series of drills. It was not Conte, nor even fitness chief Paolo Bertelli, but midfielder Arturo Vidal who was forcing his teammates to push harder and run further than they had before.

Just two months earlier, in a late-April derby against city rivals Torino, the Chilean had done much the same, driving his side forward against a determined opponent before breaking the game open with a well-struck shot from 25 yards out. That key game seemed to be headed for a draw before Vidal made that decisive intervention and the celebration would further establish the strong bond he has forged with Conte.

The player sprinted through the rain towards the bench with the coach meeting him. Both men leapt into the others arms, sharing an embrace that endured even as the rest of the team joined them. Since the two arrived at Juventus back in 2011 superlatives had rained down on the club, praising the coach for building an all-conquering team in his own image. But if this Juventus was shaped to the never-say-die attitude that has been a hallmark of Conte's career, it is Vidal who embodies that on the pitch; a living, breathing example of the Juventus spirit, which is so often the topic of discussion.

Arriving from Leverkusen after an impressive final season, his role in the team was uncertain. Images of Conte leading him by the hand through drills in his early days making front page news in Italy's sports papers. He soon made his importance clear, forcing the coach to switch from that initial 4-2-4 formation to join Claudio Marchisio and Andrea Pirlo in a well-balanced trio that swept all before it on the peninsula.

Without the distraction of European competition, a side who had disappointed since their 2007 return to Serie A, went through the entire campaign undefeated. While Pirlo's intelligent passing saw him lead Serie A with thirteen assists, it was Vidal who underpinned the side, contributing seven goals and three assists in 33 league appearances. He would earn the nickname 'Captain Hook' for a knack of chasing down opponents and scooping the ball away cleanly, but his breakout second season would see him improve almost every facet of his game and see him bestowed with a much more aptly fitting moniker.

Juve's top scorer and assist maker with ten and eight respectively, he added a further three goals in the club's return to Champions League action, raising his game in the elite competition, as the best players always seem to. Conspicuously absent from the thirty man Ballon d'Or shortlist, Vidal would again take on more responsibility in his third season and eventually become known as simply "King Arturo".

He would again dominate, perhaps most notably when FC Copenhagen visited Turin for a Champions League game the Bianconeri simply had to win if they were to hold on to any hope of qualifying for the knock-out stages. Vidal gave his side the lead from the penalty spot, only to see former Juve man Olof Mellberg scramble an equaliser. Again, the Chilean would lead the way, converting another spot kick before sealing the first hat-trick of his career with a superbly taken headed goal.

It saw Vidal join Omar Sívori, Paolo Rossi, Michael Laudrup, Alessandro Del Piero and Pippo Inzaghi as the only players in the club's history to net a European Cup treble. He went home with the match ball tucked under one arm where it would soon be joined by a new contract as he signed a deal that tied him to the club until 2017.

That was a huge fillip for the Bianconeri, further proof they have re-established themselves as one of Europe's premier sides. President Agnelli may have declared Italy is "no longer the final destination but a transit destination" for players, but Vidal seems content to call Turin home for the peak years of his career. The extension came at a perfect time for Juventus and underlined his importance to them; surprisingly the club's leading scorer in the Conte era, with a further 17 assists.

Arguably the most complete midfielder in Europe, he developed a wonderful ability to score when his side needed him most, many of his goals coming with the score at 0-0. His scoring has directly resulted in success and it was clear that the player was worth every penny of his new deal, particularly given his initial transfer cost the Bianconeri just €10 million.

That immediately looked like incredible value as King Arturo pushed this version of Juventus to be the best that it can possibly be, just as he had in those pre-season scrimmages. Yet even after two years of incredible success and with players like Vidal and Pirlo delivering their very best performances, some wiser heads remained cautious. Now captain following the departure of Del Piero, Gigi Buffon sounded the first warning, telling reporters before the season began that "it won't be easy to reclaim our title. In fact, this year will be even harder than the previous two."

A resurgent Roma would emerge in those early days of 2013-14, stirring echoes of Conte's Juve from two years previously. The Giallorossi ripped off ten consecutive wins to record an incredible start to life under new boss Rudi Garcia, posing perhaps the most consistent threat the Bianconeri had seen since their former captain returned to Turin. Their first competitive game would be the Super Coppa meeting with Lazio and Juve would use the showpiece event to lay down a marker for what was to follow.

In six devastating second half minutes, they would crush the Coppa Italia winners running out 4-0 victors. They would narrowly defeat Sampdoria before another demolition of Lazio in Turin. Week eight of the season would provide a rude awakening however as the Bianconeri – who had not lost away to Fiorentina since 1998 – somehow managed to throw away a two goal lead over the Viola. Giuseppe Rossi's hat-trick and a Joaquín strike would hand Vincenzo Montella's men a victory over their most bitter rivals.

With Conte's men eliminated from the Champions League shortly after, unable to emerge from a weak looking group, questions began to swirl over whether this team was as good as it appeared to be. They would respond in emphatic fashion by winning nine consecutive matches, a run which saw them concede just a single goal and it would see two men who had joined the club that previous summer who would begin to write their own names into the club's storied history.

Beppe Marotta had finally delivered in that July transfer window, bringing not one but two top strikers to Turin in a bid to resolve the scoring issues which had been the only blight on the two title-winning campaigns. Fernando Llorente's free transfer from Athletic Club had been followed by the £10 million acquisition of Carlos Tevez from Manchester City. Finally, Conte's Juve would have the cutting edge it had previously lacked and it would be during that victorious run that their newly discovered partnership would flourish.

Llorente, a hulking 6ft 5in striker, would firmly end the doubts which had plagued his early months in Turin. His lack of action in the first few weeks led to huge amounts of press coverage, much of it going as far as to indicate he would leave when the transfer window opened in January. Instead, the Spaniard's importance to Juventus was established as he put his lack of match fitness behind him and rewarded the effort Conte had put into teaching him the tactical system and movement expected of him.

The Basque native would prove to be far more than 'just' a goal scorer, making other telling contributions all over the pitch. His ability to hold up the ball and bring others into play was almost as invaluable as his goals and his link-up play really caught the eye as, far from merely occupying a forward role, he was everywhere, joining play and providing an essential outlet as Juventus looked to relieve pressure.

Having scored in only one of his first twelve domestic appearances, he began to register with the regularity demanded of such a headline signing. In Italy, the final minutes of games are referred to as the 'Zona Cesarini' in honour of Juventus legend Renato Cesarini, who played for the club in the 1930s when they last won three consecutive titles, and Llorente would follow in his footsteps with some vital late goals. However, Cesarini was not only part of that fine side, but he would later coach a team containing John Charles and Omar Sívori to further glory.

It was he who recommended the latter to Juventus, having coached him as a youngster with River Plate, and it was with the iconic 1960s duo who Llorente and Tevez would regularly be compared. While the Spaniard is a very different player from the gentlemanly Wales legend, the parallels between the former Manchester City captain and the devilish Sivori were much clearer.

Like the 1961 Balon d'Or winner, Tevez is a technically gifted player blessed with incredible touch, vision and an eye for goal rivalled by very few of his peers. Like his compatriot, his career to date shows Tevez can infuriate and inspire team-mates and coaches in equal measure, capable of being brilliant one moment but imploding the next, but he clearly bought into the team-first attitude of Conte and the club. There would be no sign of the drama that plagued Tevez's relationship with Roberto Mancini which resulted in the player's eventual exit from Manchester City.

Like that famed Charles-Sivori pairing, both new signings were hugely versatile players who meshed together far more than the stereotypical front pairing. A 2-0 win over Livorno in November offered insight into how well the two fit together, each getting on the score sheet with great link-up play between them, particularly given the small number of games they had started in tandem at that point. Llorente, having scored the opener, set up his partner's goal with a wonderful pass as Juve rolled on to yet another victory.

Such games displayed the absolute quality demanded by strikers at the very best clubs. Both men were known primarily as scorers and goals were undoubtedly the chief reason they were brought to Turin, yet to discuss either of them in terms of only their contribution to the scoring tally was hugely reductive. Both consummate team players, they worked tirelessly with and without the ball to help push the team to victory at both ends of the field.

The time it took for the pair to settle was fully understandable and, with them working well together, it was no surprise that the Bianconeri once again found themselves atop the Serie A standings despite Roma's own excellent form. With the two leading sides set to meet shortly after the winter break the game was built up as being hugely decisive for the title race, but it would merely serve to highlight the gulf in quality between Juve and the rest of the league.

The previously unbeaten Giallorossi were brushed aside with an emphatic 3-0 result, although Conte typically continued to urge everyone to remain focussed. "I am only ever moderately satisfied until we achieve our targets", he told reporters after the match. "This remains a stepping stone, but nothing definitive. There's an entire second half of the season to go and we must do well." They would do so with victory over Torino in the derby, before goals from Tevez and Llorente handed them an emphatic 2-0 win over an ailing Milan.

A series of slender triumphs followed, as Juventus balanced the demands of the Serie A campaign with their return to continental action in the Europa League. Single-goal wins against Fiorentina, Genoa and Catania often came as a result of individual brilliance, perhaps none more so than Andrea Pirlo's sumptuous last minute free-kick against Genoa. An incredible twenty-two match unbeaten run eventually came to an end against Napoli and Benfica would deny the Bianconeri the opportunity to win European silverware at home, eliminating them from the Europa League at the last hurdle, before they lost the final at Juventus Stadium to Sevilla.

In the end, Juventus won the title while sat watching Roma lose to Catania on television, crowned champions before they faced Atalanta the following day. They would secure a final tally of 102 points to set a new record and break Inter's 97-point mark from 2006-07, wiping yet another post-Calciopoli stain from history. Winning 33 games – including a perfect nineteen of nineteen at home – Conte would honour his players by telling a press conference that "these lads tore up records upon records and people will talk about this Juventus side for a long time to come."

This truly was an incredible side, one which proved their domestic supremacy and one which could go on to achieve even greater success in the future. Antonio Conte had reinvigorated Juventus, taking her from abject mediocrity and back to the very summit of Italian football.

Then just like that, it was over. Antonio Conte's resignation as Juventus manager arrived like a lightning strike, the first whispers leaking less than fifteen minutes before the club confirmed the 44 year old had quit. Later, a recorded interview from Conte confirmed his own departure just two days into pre-season training ahead of the 2014-15 campaign. An open letter from President Andrea Agnelli attempted to console ailing supporters, thanking Conte for the "three years in which we rewrote this club's history" and noting that the news had "saddened him greatly."

Supporters felt exactly the same way, deeply shocked that the man responsible for transforming La Madama back into a serial winner was gone. The President's statement went on to say that "Juventus must continue on its path," and indeed she must, the loss of the manager simply another obstacle for the Bianconeri to overcome in what has always been relentless pursuit of glory. While it appears Conte's pathological desire to win had left him exhausted and unable to carry on, the club reacted quickly and appointed Massimiliano Allegri the very next day. Fans protested outside the club's training ground as the new manager held his inaugural press conference, angry at the former Milan boss taking a seat on the nation's most prestigious bench.

Yet even the new boss knew the quickest way to appease their fears was simple, telling reporters at his inaugural press conference that he understood the skepticism of the supporters, vowing to "win them over with results, hard work, respect and professionalism." Allegri instantly recognised that there is one burning question that remains is one that follows La Madama wherever she goes, and that is to see whether she can collect trophies with a regularity to live up to Boniperti's comment from all those years ago.

It remains as true today as it was back then because, at Juventus, winning truly is the only thing that counts.

FOREVER ENTWINED: JUVENTUS & THE AZZURRI

The history of Juventus and the Italian national team are so entwined that sometimes it seems the two are almost inseparable. Their respective peaks and troughs often mirror one another, with Italy's moments of triumph always arriving when the squad is based around the peninsula's most famous club. Indeed, seven of the top ten most capped Azzurri internationals have been at Juventus at some point of their careers.

The two main reasons for this trend are extremely simple. Firstly, Juventus is Italy's most successful club by far. Secondly, the club has a tradition of comprising a squad made up largely of homegrown players. The twenty-five-man squad in 2012-13 contained no fewer than sixteen Italians. That is in line with previous seasons as the Bianconeri have always maintained that Italian core, with a number of naturalised players such as Omar Sívori, Mauro Camoranesi and Amauri often adding to the tally.

Overall, Juventus is the club that has contributed the most players to the Italian national team in history, with 123 Bianconeri players featuring in competitive games for Italy. They also boast a formidable twenty-two Italians who were at the club when they lifted the World Cup, a record for any club in world football. In addition to this, Zinedine Zidane and Didier Deschamps won the World Cup for France while playing at Juventus.

The most recent World Cup Final appearance by the Azzurri – in 2006 against France – featured no less than nine Juventus players. Two players, Salvatore 'Toto' Schillaci and Paolo Rossi, won the Golden Boot as top scorer, in the 1990 and 1982 editions of the competition respectively. While only three Juventus players were part of Italy's European Championship triumph in 1968, three more have won the competition with another nation. Luis del Sol won it in 1964 with Spain, while Frenchmen Zidane (2000) and Michel Platini (1984) matched that feat, the latter also ending his run by being named the tournament's top scorer.

It is abundantly clear that during every moment of triumph for the Azzurri, there have always been significant contributions from men belonging to La Vecchia Signora. From Gianpiero Combi and

Felice Borel in the 1930s, through the legendary Gaetano Scirea, Dino Zoff, Antonio Cabrini and of course Marco Tardelli in 1982 to Gigi Buffon, Alessandro Del Piero and Gianluca Zambrotta in 2006. It is no surprise that in the four years where Italy has lifted the ultimate prize, the Bianconeri have won the Scudetto.

What is less apparent, however, is that the reverse is also often the case. Some of Italy's worst showings at a World Cup tournament have coincided with Juventus suffering some of their own worst seasons. In South Africa in 2010, a dire Azzurri squad was sent home after the first round, eliminated without winning a single match as they finished bottom of a weak group containing New Zealand, Slovakia and Paraguay. It is not difficult to remember that in the two seasons either side of that disaster, Juventus limped to consecutive seventh place finishes in Serie A and looked every inch as poor as the national team did.

Again looking back through history, the pattern repeats itself; in 1954 the Azzurri were eliminated in the first round of a competition sandwiched between second and seventh place Serie A finishes from Juventus. A worse fate befell Italy four years later when they failed to even qualify the tournament, an abysmal campaign which encompassed seventh, twelfth and ninth placed finishes for the Turin-based giants. In subsequent competitions – held in 1962 and 1966 – the Bianconeri ended the season in fifth and twelfth place respectively as Italy again crashed out in the first round. The latter of those – hosted by England – saw perhaps the most infamous Azzurri loss ever as Pak Doo-Ik handed North Korea a 1-0 win at Middlesbrough's Ayresome Park.

So while Juventus and her supporters have always been quick to champion their club's influence on the national team in times of glory, they must also accept that the Azzurri have been a mirror image of the less than vintage Bianconeri teams in Italy's darkest hours. Yet, it seems even those can unite the two and never was this more apparent than during the 2006 World Cup. Just as it had 24 years earlier when Paolo Rossi's return from the ban he suffered as a result of the Totonero scandal, the lingering thought of how Calciopoli would affect their careers forged an Italy side that would prove unbreakable.

"When a team is attacked, it makes them perform miracles."
– Paolo Rossi

Italy's entire preparation for the tournament in Germany was overshadowed by the news of wrongdoing by so many of Serie A's biggest clubs, with the players facing endless questions about how the events unfolding would impact their training. Fabio Cannavaro and Gianluigi Buffon were both interrogated as part of the investigation while the coach's own son – Davide Lippi – was implicated due to the GEA World agency which he ran with Moggi's son, Alessandro.

Yet, despite it all, Marcello Lippi adhered to his original plan. He called five Juventus players, selecting all but one in the opening game against the Czech Republic. No fewer than thirteen members of the squad were drawn from the four clubs implicated in the match-fixing scandal. They faced the ultimate football dichotomy as they went to the World Cup proudly representing their nation, the whole time knowing that when they returned they might well be looking for new employers following the demotion of their clubs.

Italy won that game comfortably and by the time they had reached the quarter-finals – recording wins over Ghana and Australia along the way – they had grown into an incredibly close group. Their collective reaction to Francesco Totti's last minute penalty in the latter of those ties was not only one of elation and relief, but also showed just how events at home had become a source of inspiration.

Lippi, as he had in two spells with Juventus, used the scandal to create a siege mentality around the squad. He didn't need much encouragement to convince the players that only by pulling together and winning, could they be judged solely by what happened on the field of play. That freedom saw a remarkably more attacking side than any Azzurri display in recent memory, as they tore into opponents the way the Bianconeri did during the coach's first spell in Turin.

As if any reminder of how serious events were at home were needed, captain Cannavaro received one in the worst of circumstances. Relaxed and laughing his way through a press conference ahead of the quarter-final, news broke that Gianluca Pessotto – by then in an administrative role with Juventus – had attempted suicide at the club's training ground. He survived the fall, but the effect the news had on his former teammates was soon evident. With both the mental and physical condition of their friend added to the start of the Calciopoli trials, Italy demolished an over-matched Ukraine team 3-0 with Gianluca Zambrotta – Pessotto's long time roommate at Juventus – scoring a wonderful goal. At full-time he unfurled an Italian flag with the message 'Pessottino we are with you' written across it for everyone to see.

"My goal was for him", the fullback – who along with Ciro Ferrara and Alessandro Del Piero immediately flew home to visit Pessotto in hospital – told reporters. "All the squad wants to extend an affectionate hug to him." They took that same camaraderie into the semi-final with Germany on the very same day that Prosecutor Stefano Palazzi recommended Juventus should be relegated to Serie C2, the fourth division of Italian football. Playing with incredible spirit, despite so many of the squad not knowing where their futures lay, the Azzurri won the game with late goals from Fabio Grosso and Del Piero. The belief of the players was evident in a match that ranks among the very best in history and the emotional outpouring and relief that greeted the first strike will perhaps never be matched.

In the final they would meet a France team boasting Lilian Thuram and David Trezeguet, both of Juventus, among their stars, adding further significance to the fixture. The final swung on one key incident between two men on the score-sheet as Zinedine Zidane, formerly of Juventus, became involved in a dispute with Marco Materazzi. The talismanic French captain inexplicably head-butted the Italian in the chest and, after referee Horacio Elizondo was informed of the incident, the Argentine was left with no choice but to send Zidane off. His shell-shocked teammates held on to force penalties for only the second time in World Cup Final history, but Pirlo, Materazzi, Daniele de Rossi, Del Piero and Grosso made no mistake as Italy became the most successful European country in World Cup history.

A triumphant Italy would return home, feted wherever they went, with the players sealing their places in both history and the hearts of the nation. "If the scandal hadn't happened I think we wouldn't have won the World Cup", said Milan midfielder Gennaro Gattuso. "It has given us more strength. This squad showed great heart and maybe it wasn't pretty, but we were hard to beat. We played it one game at a time and with great humility."

Juventus may have suffered as the aftermath of Calciopoli broke up the team and resigned them to six years of footballing purgatory, but for that wonderful summer of 2006 the peninsula's greatest sporting-related scandal was the driving force in a victory that will never be forgotten. Juventus and Italy truly are inseparable, for better and for worse.

ACKNOWLEDGMENTS

The author would like to thank the following people, without whose contributions and assistance this book could not have been written;

Claudio Albanese, Michael Atkinson, David Amoyal, Sheridan Bird, John Cascarano, Gino De Blasio (for always being there when needed), John Dobson, David Hartrick, Kristian Jack, Jeff Livingstone, James Montague, Robert Priest, Giancarlo Rinaldi (for his insight and encouragement), Carey Roberts and Aaron West.

Grazie mille e un abbraccio forte a tutti!

REFERENCES

Pg 8:
The 'Caso Rosetta'
museodelcalcio.it/new_catalogo/Default5.html

Pg 10:
The 'Metodo System' 'Inverting the Pyramid: A history of football tactics" by Jonathan Wilson

Pg 16:
Delle Alpi average attendance and Sampdoria game attendance
theguardian.com/football/2006/mar/19/sport.comment1

Pg 18:
Napoli stadium costs and revenue received
swissramble.blogspot.co.uk/2011/04/napolis-success-story.html

Pg 18:
Costs of Juventus Stadium
juventus.com/wps/portal/it/stadio/stadio/progetto/ideahttp://www.ilnuovostadiodellajuventus.com/Pages/i_numeri.aspx

and naming rights sold to SportFive
sportfive.com/index.php?id=385

Pg 22:
Giovanni De Luna on Juventus fans, name not place
tuttosport.com/calcio/2014/04/12-291458/Ecco+perch%C3%A9+la+Juve+o+la+si+ama+o+la+si+odia

Pg 25:
Edoardo Agnelli charged with possession of heroin:
"Mondo Agnelli: Fiat, Chrysler, and the Power of a Dynasty" by Jennifer Clark

Pg 42:
The Makelele Role
independent.co.uk/sport/football/news-and-comment/doing-a-makelele--so-good-they-named-it-after-him-437647.html

Pg 44:
"The Damned United" by David Peace

Pg 51:
Visiting San Mames in 1977 *http://www.storiedicalcio.altervista.org/juve_uefa_1977.html*

Pg 57:
Paolo Rossi suspension "Il pallone truccato. L'illecito nel calcio italiano" by Paolo Carbone

Pg 66:
Heysel account
bbc.co.uk/news/10176462

Pg 70:
Scirea & Zoff: Switzerland
repubblica.it/2009/05/rubriche/la-storia/zoff-scirea/zoff-scirea.html

Pg 82:
Alfred Dick and the birth of Torino FC
torinofc.it/storia_loader_contenuto/1825

Pg 84:
Ian Rush surprised by 5,000 at Turin airport
observer.theguardian.com/osm/story/0,,1404050,00.html

Pg 87:
Roberto Baggio turning to Buddhism
soccertranslator.com/2014/05/world-cup-legends-excerpts-from-una.html

Pg 88:
Gigi Maifredi & 'Champagne football'
*archiviostorico.corriere.it/2001/febbraio/18/Maifredi_fantasma_
del_calcio_champagne_co_0_0102188386.shtml*

Pg 98:
Andrea Fortunato leucemia and death *http://archivio.
lastampa.it/LaStampaArchivio/main/History/tmpl_viewObj.
jsp?objid=1251736*

Pg 102:
Del Piero-Inzaghi relationship
*archiviostorico.corriere.it/2002/settembre/23/Del_Piero_
Inzaghi_divisi_tutto_co_0_02092310987.shtml*

Pg 103: Massimo Mauro fight in Parliament, 1998
itnsource.com/shotlist//RTV/1998/04/30/804290009/?s=leftist

Pg 111: Collina performance Venezia-Roma *http://www.
repubblica.it/online/calcio/morfuria/morfuria/morfuria.html*

Pg 123: Initial Calciopoli verdicts
ft.com/cms/s/2/6129251e-0de3-11db-a385-0000779e2340.html

Pg 125:
Definitions of Article One,
Six & 18 of FIGC Code of Sporting Justice
*lawinsport.com/blog/italian-sports-law-blog/item/
illegal-betting-and-match-fixing-in-italy*

Pg 126:
Calciopoli II 'Forza Italia: The Fall and Rise of Italian Football' by
Paddy Agnew

Pg 176:
Andrea Agnelli appointment, equal punishments
ft.com/cms/s/2/8767cc64-ad44-11e2-b27f-00144feabdc0.html

A huge thanks also goes to the extensive archives of Gazzetta dello Sport, La Repubblica and La Stampa, as well as 'Calcio' by John Foot, 'Forza Italia: The Fall and Rise of Italian Football' by Paddy Agnew and 'King John: John Charles The Autobiography' by John Charles with Bob Harris, all of which were invaluable resources regarding various details of the history of Juventus.